Educational Leadership
Key Challenges and Ethical Tensions

Educational Leadership: Key Challenges and Ethical Tensions is a major new work on contemporary leadership challenges for educational leaders. Based on groundbreaking research, this book provides educational leaders in schools – including teachers – with ways of analysing and resolving ethically complex issues. The ethical tensions inherent in common leadership challenges are identified; a framework for their analysis presented and explained; and a clear, practitioner-focused method for ethical decision-making recommended.

Written by a leading researcher in the field, and recipient of the Australian Council for Educational Leadership Gold Medal for excellence, *Educational Leadership* is an important book that provides a practical approach to improving leadership through a greater understanding of ethical concepts and theories, presented, explained and applied to real-life tensions in practitioner language. Furthermore, *Educational Leadership* challenges current paradigms of leadership training and development, suggesting a new approach using formation processes based on leadership capabilities.

Professor Patrick Duignan BA, H Dip ED (NUI) B.Ed, M.Ed.Admin, Ph.D. (ALTA)
Patrick is Foundation Chair in Educational Leadership and Director of the Flagship for Creative & Authentic Leadership at Australian Catholic University.

Educational Leadership

Key Challenges and Ethical Tensions

PATRICK DUIGNAN

CAMBRIDGE
UNIVERSITY PRESS

CAMBRIDGE UNIVERSITY PRESS
Cambridge, New York, Melbourne, Madrid, Cape Town, Singapore, São Paulo

Cambridge University Press
477 Williamstown Road, Port Melbourne, VIC 3207, Australia

Published in the United States of America by Cambridge University Press, New York

www.cambridge.org
Information on this title: www.cambridge.org/9780521685122

© Patrick Duignan 2006

First published 2006

Reprinted 2007, 2008

Printed in China by Everbest Printing Company Limited

A catalogue record for this publication is available from the British Library

National Library of Australia Cataloguing in Publication data

   Duignan, P. A. (Patrick Augustine)
   Educational Leadership: Key Challenges and Ethical Tensions
   Bibliography.
   Includes index.
   ISBN-13 978-0-521-68512-2 paperback
   ISBN-10 0-521-68512-5 paperback
   1. Educational leadership – Australia.   2. Educational leadership – Moral and ethical
   aspects – Australia.   3. School administrators – Professional ethics – Australia.
   4. Decision-making – Moral and ethical aspects.   I. Title.
371.200994

To Nuala, our children, and grandchildren

Contents

Acknowledgements

Parts of this book are based on a three-year research project, 'Contemporary challenges and implications for leaders in frontline human service organisations', funded by the Australian Research Council (ARC). As Chief Investigator of this research, I recognise and appreciate their support.

I owe a big thank you to a number of people.

The research report was written by Patrick Duignan (Chief Investigator), Charles Burford, Mary Cresp, Tony d'Arbon, Michael Fagan, Mary Frangoulis, Michael Gorman, Ron Ikin, Aengus Kavanagah, Marilyn Kelleher, Soma Nagappan, and Michael Walsh. Victoria Collins and Lyn Coulon were valued members of the research team.

A special thanks to Michael Walsh, who gave permission to adapt his material on values and ethics from the research report. Also to Ron Ikin, who gave advice on an early version of this book.

To Soma Nagappan, a friend and colleague, thanks for your valuable assistance and advice. Thank you, Trish, for your patience and expertise in typing numerous drafts of the manuscript, and Kristan for your specialist advice.

Of course, without the love, advice and support of my spouse, Nuala, over our many great years together, this book, as well as many other adventures, would not have been possible. Thank you for your careful reading of the manuscript and your insightful and valued advice.

I have learned a great deal over many years from our three children, Siobhan, Patrick and Finola and, of course more recently, from their spouses Christopher, Fiona, and Michael.

Our grandchildren, Matthew, Benjamin, Joe, Conor, Cormac, and Molly Kate are the light of our lives. We are indeed blessed.

Thanks to Cambridge University Press for believing in the book, and a special thanks to my extraordinarily supportive, wise and expert editor, Helena Bond.

Introduction and overview

Educational leaders are confronted by external and internal challenges and expectations that make considerable demands on their time, expertise, energies and emotional wellbeing. Increasingly, they are being held accountable for both performance and compliance with ethical and moral standards in their relationships and practices.

While leaders may experience confusion, even frustration, in attempting to respond productively to these challenges, many other organisational members feel used, even devalued, by the current emphasis on corporate management values, strategies and practices in many educational organisations. Many educational leaders are faced with tensions between the demands of managerialism (efficiency, productivity, accountability) and the expectations created within a values-based school community. This perception of 'excessive managerialism' has led to a call for the transformation of managers and administrators into leaders who focus more on people-related issues in organisations (Little, 1997).

This book is written within a leadership context that is increasingly sensitive to the need for sound ethical and moral standards in how organisations are led and decisions made. The recent lapses in ethical and moral judgements by leaders in worldwide organisations such as WorldCom and Enron – as well as HIH, James Hardie Industries and the Australian Wheat Board in Australia – have heightened leaders' awareness of the necessity of maintaining high standards of ethical behaviour in their organisations. I believe that many of the leaders who have recently had to stand trial for their misadventures lacked basic appreciation of the need for ethical and moral standards in their actions and transactions.

While similar scandals have not been so publicly apparent in education, it would seem to be an opportune time for educational leaders to ensure that they are embedding high ethical and moral standards in their policies and practices.

About this book

The primary purpose for writing this book is to provide educational leaders, including teachers, with ways of analysing the challenges they face, including the ethical tensions inherent in many of these challenges. Methods for educational leaders to analyse the ethical dimensions in the challenges they face are described and analysed. A values- and ethics-based approach for making decisions in situations fraught with paradox and ambiguity is also discussed.

There is also a strong recommendation that those in formal leadership positions must: share leadership responsibilities by building the leadership capacity of all stakeholders; develop their leadership capabilities so as to be able to share these leadership responsibilities; become more capable as authentic human beings in order to become more capable as leaders; and be better 'formed' and informed as leaders to meet the challenges and tensions discussed in chapters 2 and 3.

This book has a number of characteristics that make it useful for both researching and practising leadership:

1 It is a research-based book (three-year government-funded project) on leadership challenges and the ethical issues faced by contemporary educational leaders.
2 It identifies and analyses many of these challenges as tensions that normally have no *either/or*, *right/wrong* solutions.
3 The challenges discussed and analysed usually involve people contesting values or perspectives.
4 A framework is presented to assist leaders to analyse these challenges and tensions.
5 A clear and practitioner-focused set of guidelines and a method for making decisions that involve ethical tensions, including a generally jargon-free discussion of ethical theories and principles, is presented and explained.

6 A case is made for educational leaders to develop their leadership capabilities as well as their leadership and management competencies.

7 A shared, authentic approach to educational leadership is recommended as most appropriate and effective for educational leaders who are required to make ethical decisions in situations of tension and paradox.

8 A framework is proposed for the preparation and development of authentic leaders, focusing on leadership capabilities and using a 'formation' approach – the philosophy of this approach emphasises, first and foremost, that educational leaders need to be 'formed' as capable and authentic human beings who can engage in mature and productive ways with all key stakeholders in order to build leadership capacity in their schools.

The book is organised around the following chapters.

The argument in chapter 1 suggests that educational leaders, like leaders in most organisations today, both public and private, are influenced by global and societal trends and pressures. A growing trend towards 'intense individualism' and an increasing disengagement of the self from a sense of the collective seems to cause many to focus on selfish and addictive ways of living and working. Schools may be contributing to the development of these addictive ways and, therefore, it is the ethical and social responsibility of educational leaders to create the type of learning environments in their schools that will assist students to develop a healthier balance between their individual interests and the common good.

An added challenge for educational leaders is that there seems to be a growing cynicism in the public arena concerning the honesty and integrity of many contemporary leaders, especially those in business and politics. In recent years, there have been calls for leaders to demonstrate greater moral purpose, ethical competence, and authenticity in their actions and relationships. Much of the argument in this book attempts to assist educational leaders to respond to complex, uncertain and tension-filled challenges in ethical, moral and authentic ways.

A brief overview of the research underpinning a number of the discussions in this book is provided at the end of chapter 1.

In chapter 2, a number of key leadership challenges, derived from a three-year research study, are reported and discussed. These challenges are identified as:

1 providing a values-driven vision for the future;
2 managing staff relationships;
3 leading people;
4 balancing personal and professional responsibilities;
5 communicating effectively;
6 leading continuous change;
7 managing accountability and individual performance; and
8 leading an ageing workforce.

In chapter 3, it is argued that many of the contemporary challenges faced by educational leaders involve complex and often conflicting human relationships, as well as a contestation of values. Such challenges can be legitimately described as tensions. A number of these tensions are explained using accompanying short cases, and lessons for educational leaders are proposed from this analysis.

In chapter 4, a framework is developed and explained for analysing these tensions. This framework will assist educational leaders to identify the multiple perspectives and value positions that participants bring to contentious problems. The framework, based on the notion of a double-headed arrow, supports the view that the inclusion of competing value perspectives, within a *both/and* mindset, is usually essential for successful ethical decision-making.

In chapter 5, a values and ethics approach to making decisions in situations of paradox and tension is described, discussed and explained. A special emphasis is placed on the importance of ethics in decision-making, and different approaches to ethics are explained and critiqued. The rationale for a method of ethical decision-making is also developed.

In chapter 6, a method for ethical decision-making, taking into consideration the reality of the contexts within which educational leaders work, is described and explained. The method provides educational leaders with practical guidelines for ethical decision-making.

In chapter 7, educational leaders are advised to build cultures of shared and distributed leadership in their schools. It is arguably an ethical responsibility of formal educational leaders to enable key stakeholders to share in the leadership responsibilities of their school community. Nominated leaders are particularly advised to assist teachers to become more involved in key decisions relating to learning and teaching, and to regard themselves as key educational leaders in their school communities.

In chapter 8, it is argued that for educational leaders to lead ethically in an age of uncertainty and unpredictable change, they need, first and foremost, to be capable human beings. The competency-based approach to leader development is critiqued and a framework based on leadership capabilities is recommended.

In chapter 9, the concept of authentic leadership is explored and is linked to authentic learning and teaching. It is suggested that we need authentic educational leaders in our schools. The ethics of authenticity, responsibility and presence (Starratt, 2004a) are introduced and discussed.

In chapter 10, a case is made for leadership preparation and development programs to adopt a 'formation approach', or, better still, a formation philosophy, processes and content. Such formation programs should engage participants in ethical reasoning and in developing 'wisdom ways of knowing' (Groome, 1998). The concept of leader formation is explained and key capabilities of effective educational leaders are identified and explained. A philosophy and some modes of delivery for a leadership formation program are then suggested.

At the end of each chapter is a section of 'Key ideas for reflection', which suggests a number of relevant ideas for the reader's further consideration and raises some questions for reflection.

Chapter 1

Contemporary leaders and leadership under the spotlight

In this chapter I will examine aspects of the environments within which educational leaders operate. These environments are extremely complex and would require a whole book to do them justice. For the purposes of this book, with its primary focus on ethical and moral leadership, I will examine selected aspects of these environments, which I suggest may impact on the way in which educational leaders exercise their choices and make their decisions.

Educational leaders live and work in a global world that, according to Giddens (1998), influences social processes and institutions and encourages new forms of individualism that contribute to more selfish modes of living. Slavish commitment to individualised ways of living can generate addictions, especially process addictions, that are so pervasive that we may not even be aware of them. A disturbing implication of these process addictions is that they start very early in life and schools may wittingly or unwittingly encourage them in students. In a century characterised by enormous choices, it would be somewhat ironic if schools prepared students more for addiction than for choice.

Educational leaders and teachers have a particular responsibility to ensure that students in their care receive the type of education and learning experiences that help transform their lives so that they can break the bonds imposed by forces for 'intense individualism' (Sommerville, 2000) and better contribute, as responsible citizens, to the common good. *Educational* leaders need to be socially as well as educationally responsible, in order to create the conditions within their schools that challenge students to see the bigger picture and to want to make a difference in their own lives and in the larger community. As is suggested throughout this book, effective educational leaders have an ethical responsibility to optimise learning opportunities and outcomes for their students by helping create organisational learning environments that are visionary, authentic, ethical, strategic, people-centred and motivational.

Unfortunately too many leaders, especially those in politics and the business world, have not lived up to such expectations in recent times. Many in our communities doubt the credibility, especially with regard to ethical and moral standards, of leaders of many of our public and private institutions. Numerous examples of leaders deliberately taking actions that lack ethical and moral content have led to a public culture of cynicism about leaders and leadership.

And yet I believe that there is some good news. For a variety of reasons, there is a growing public chorus demanding ethical and authentic leadership. These demands are raising the ethical and moral bar for contemporary leaders. The future is looking somewhat brighter.

Globalisation, intense individualism and addictions

We live in a world of 'intense individualism' (Sommerville, 2000) where selfish and self-serving means are often used to achieve ends that are inimical to community values and the common good. A slavish commitment to intense individualism can rob us of a sense of what it means to be more fully engaged with our fellow human beings. The steady growth in self-centred modes of living can diminish us as moral agents in the pursuit of the common good. In fact, it is likely that there is a connection between these contemporary individualistic tendencies and a growing indifference to communitarian justice and equality.

A selfish and materialistic way of life can, in fact, become an addiction which reflects or perhaps contributes to more widespread, even global, addictive processes. It is not only individuals in society who can become addicted, or who contribute to these addictive processes: a number of our societal agencies and institutions, including schools, may also be part of the problem.

In his groundbreaking book *The third way*, Giddens (1998, p. 33) suggested that globalisation is a complex range of processes and events driven, primarily, by '. . . a mixture of political and economic influences'. It touches all our lives, transforming our social processes and institutions, even the ways in which we relate to one another. It is this latter perspective on globalisation that is of most interest here, because as Giddens (1998, p. 33) so clearly pointed out, globalisation is '. . . directly relevant to the rise of . . . the "new individualism" . . .'.

It would seem that globalisation, especially its secular and materialistic dimensions, is contributing to a more disengaged mode of existence for many people, especially in the developed world; a condition that tends to '. . . empty life of its richness, depth, or meaning' (Taylor, 1989, p. 500).

Some are suggesting that our isolationist and self-centred ways are causing us to grasp at more temporary and ultimately less fulfilling forms of engagement, and the gradual disengagement of the self from a sense of the collective can lead to the development of a selective blindness for the plight of others less fortunate than ourselves, to the point where it can become entrenched at many levels of society. Many contemporary secular Western societies '. . . are based on *intense individualism* . . .' (Sommerville 2000, p. 5, italics in original). While this focus can lead to a sense of isolation and disengagement, humans need community for their identity, even their survival. In fact, for many, belonging to community helps give meaning and purpose to life.

Some also warn of the consequences of this love affair with ourselves. They argue that 'the ethic of individual self-fulfilment and achievement is the most powerful current in modern society', and the choosing, self-driven individual is 'the central character of our time' (Beck & Beck-Gernsheim, 2002, p. 22). Individualised modes of living have the potential to spawn a host of addict-making processes or process addictions, which are destructive of collective and communitarian interests. Process addictions, for example working long hours, stressful jobs, winning at all cost, spending beyond our means, are often applauded by society (Breton & Largent, 1996, p. 2).

These addictions are so pervasive that we may not even be aware of their sometimes disastrous effects. While we are acutely familiar with the effects of substance addictions, which may directly or indirectly affect our lives, Breton and Largent (1996, p. 3) argue that process addictions are '. . . the invisible killers, the ones we don't suspect'. A key point is that these process addictions, in fact, may become invisible to us because they are so familiar.

Perhaps the most sinister influence of these process addictions is that they are promoted and supported by society at large and by its key institutions. Our schools, churches, media – even our workplaces – can create feelings of dependency in us (Breton & Largent, 1996, p. 4). Many of society's systems, structures and processes erode our sense of worth and wellbeing, create dependency, and cause us to forget the bigger communitarian picture because of our dependency on, even addiction to, materialistic, competitive, self-aggrandising habits. Too many seem to lose perspective on the need for a healthy life-giving balance between work and family and succumb to workaholic processes and career-driven ambitions.

Perhaps the most serious concern I have is that these addictive tendencies may very well start early in life, even during school years. This raises the issue of the potential role of schools in contributing to the development of these addictive tendencies and processes in children. Do schools prepare young people to choose a healthy life–work balance and develop a sense of responsibility for community values and processes? How well do schools prepare their students to develop ethical and moral frameworks that will help give purpose and meaning to their lives? Are they actually contributing directly to the growth of the addictive-type processes just discussed?

The role of schools

As we begin a millennium of choices, we need to ask how well schools prepare students to choose morally, ethically and wisely. We may, in fact, be failing our young people in our schools and in our learning frameworks and processes. Much learning in schools is based on regurgitation of facts in tests, without children knowing why their answers are deemed to be correct. Such 'inauthentic' learning does not generally prepare students for things that will be meaningful in their lives, and is primarily focused on passing the tests that are used to determine how well they can pass these tests (Starratt, 2004a, p. 57). Such competitive pressures seem to be pushing students towards selfish, individualised, overly competitive attitudes and behaviours.

A sobering consequence of such inauthentic approaches to teaching and learning is that at least some schools may be preparing students more for addiction than for making worthwhile choices in their lives (Breton & Largent, 1996, p. 4). John Taylor Gatto (1992), in his book *Dumbing us down: The hidden curriculum of compulsory schooling*, reflects on the possible negative consequences of the messages some schools give to their students, primarily through their structures and processes. As principal of a secondary school, he concluded that the tight schedules (timetables), switching from classroom to classroom in response to ringing bells, and the constant 'surveillance' (reminiscent of prisons) seemed to be designed to prevent children from developing independence and, in fact, was coaxing them into 'addiction and dependent behaviour' (p. xii).

It may be, therefore, that current assumptions about teaching and learning, as well as the structures that are deeply embedded in much of contemporary schooling, need to be challenged (Duignan, 2004a). Despite protestations from educational professionals to the contrary, it would seem that far too many schools, especially secondary schools, still operate using traditional structures and modes of delivery more suited to pre-technological or pre-twenty-first century ways of thinking and doing. Many schools are locked into compartmentalised structures for learning based on reductionist models of knowledge, i.e. subjects and departments.

Such structures and approaches fail to take into consideration the holistic and integrating nature of knowledge for the lives of learners, and the role of schools in the spiritual and moral development of students. The most destructive part of the hidden curriculum for students is that they have been 'trained to give up a great deal of personal power' and they experience a 'profound sense of disenfranchisement' (Fourre, 2003, p. 77). While recommending a greater commitment to justice, she cautioned that a deep sense of social responsibility can only be applied to life by those who possess a sense 'of their own power and their responsibility to use it for good' (p. 77).

This negative view of schools and schooling presents a challenge for educational leaders, who have a particular responsibility to use learning opportunities to promote the good of students as well as that of the community. They need to regard it as their ethical responsibility to promote and support policies and practices in their schools that better prepare students to be faithful and responsible citizens who will not just accept the world as it is but will help transform their communities into havens of hope, promise and living witnesses of the common good. Duignan *et al.* (2005), in a three-year research project entitled 'Socially responsible indicators for policy, practice and benchmarking in service organisations', concluded that 'social responsibility is, above all, fostered by the commitment of leaders to the mission of the organisation' (p. 54), and the mission of service organisations, such as schools, usually focuses on the people side of the organisation and on the capacity of leaders to be 'ethically responsible'. In other words, providing students with learning environments that engage them fully in their own learning is an ethical challenge for educational leaders.

Leadership and social responsibility

Selznick (1992, p. 345) pointed out that to be responsible means more than being accountable. To be accountable, he suggested, is to be 'subject to judgement or, as we sometimes say, to be *held* responsible', which reflects a response to external standards. In his view, responsibility actually requires '. . . an *inner* commitment to moral restraint and aspiration'. He is critical of many of the contemporary destructive effects of intense individualism and moral indifference in our Western societies and bemoans 'the social costs of moral indifference – distorted priorities, defrauded consumers, degraded environments, deformed babies' (p. 345).

What he suggested, by implication, is that leaders need to challenge unethical and immoral policies and practices wherever they find them. Leaders, especially, must challenge the morality and validity of ingrained patterns of inequality. Accepting that many educational leaders may not be in a position to change the root causes or to remove or reshape inequitable structures and processes, they should, at the very least, name the offending issues and register their dissent. Rhetoric alone, however, is unlikely to have much impact on ingrained prejudices and taken-for-granted patterns of power, influence and relationships. Ethical action is called for.

Of course, taking such action involves courage, and ethically responsible educational leaders require great courage. In his address 'The courage to lead' (in Heft & Bennett, 2004), Heft singled out two areas of leadership in which he argued that contemporary leaders must do better – *justice* and *diversity*. In discussing the need for leaders to have the courage to lead for greater justice in society, he argued that while leaders of schools will want their graduates to succeed, this success should not mean that they fit neatly into an already unjust society but that they transform it for the common good.

In relation to diversity, often referred to as multiculturalism, Heft also cautions that some approaches by leaders '. . . are based on a false idea of tolerance' (2004, p. 17) that actually avoids commitment to principles and ethical standards. They are, in other words, lacking in moral courage. Tolerance and civility shouldn't be characterised by 'moral ambivalence', which can quickly lead to moral indifference, but by moral courage (Keane, 2003, p. 199). On the other hand, arrogant adherence to absolute values or fixed principles can lead to self-righteous behaviour. A basic ethic of tolerance, based on mutual respect for differences enshrined within a global civil society, is one way of striking a balance between bland tolerance and self-righteous behaviour (Keane, 2003).

Educational leaders, too, need to strike this balance. To assist them in doing so, I propose that they adopt the following practices:
• critique and challenge assumptions and taken-for-granted norms that condone or encourage injustices and inequalities;
• intervene to challenge inequities (material and attitudinal), even in the face of majority opposition;
• use power as a moral force for the common good;
• connect leadership to pedagogical principles that promote and support authentic learning and teaching;
• serve others through leadership practices that are collaborative and inclusive; and
• make ethical and socially responsible behaviour key parts of leadership.

Educational leaders need an ethical platform for action that will help schools steer a course away from intense individualistic and addictive practices, towards more ethical, moral and communitarian processes and actions. A concern for many people today, however, is that they perceive that many of our leaders do not follow ethical standards or act in socially responsible ways. In fact, there is widespread cynicism about the credibility and authenticity of leaders in many public and private institutions.

Cynicism about leaders and leadership

Why is there such widespread doubt in the community about the credibility of many so-called leaders in our organisations and in public life? Cynicism is a dominating theme in post-modern life and can be summed up in a series of 'don'ts': Don't trust the government. Don't trust the banks. Don't trust salespeople. Don't trust the police. Don't trust your emotions or, for that matter, your reason. Don't trust language. And most disturbing of all, don't trust yourself (Starratt, 2003, p. 51).

In collegiate settings in the United States, Bogue (1994, pp. 6–7) criticised the fact that most college administrators stand for nothing, and are frequently the cause of their own demise because of their '. . . disappointing displays of ignorance, irresponsibility, and insensitivity' and because they abandon their integrity. He argues from his review of research and literature, as well as from his own experiences, that the disappointing record of many college leaders can be traced to their flawed sense of vision, heart, spirit and character (p. 7).

His indictment of collegiate leaders is concerning, as we expect leaders in institutes of higher learning to stand for something and to help model the way for others. Perhaps he is greatly overstating the case, but there has been sufficient criticism of leaders along these lines in the public media in recent years to suggest that there is more than a grain of truth in these criticisms.

It may be more productive, however, to try to identify the possible reasons why some leaders today behave in the superficial fashion described by Bogue. I have already discussed the pressures derived from globalisation and the widespread addiction to intense individualism with its potential for self-serving modes of behaviour. A complicating factor is that most leaders have insufficient understanding of the dynamics and complexity of organisations, and instead cling to a more readily understood view of their organisations as linear, deterministic and mechanistic systems. This causes them to adopt views of management that are based on hierarchical structures and 'power over people' approaches to relationships. Such structures of 'domination', according to Starratt (1994, p. 64), prevail in our organisations and produce '. . . unjust and depersonalising relationships among individuals and among groups'. These dominant individuals or groups assume ownership of ideas and processes and act in ways that imply that they deserve to be served by, and receive deference from, others.

As already suggested, the promotion of corporate–managerialist philosophies and practices tends to support and encourage competitive and individualistic corporate cultures. Too frequently, such cultures reward naked ambition and manipulation, and emphasise self-serving practices and the importance of role and structure over ethical and authentic behaviour. Many people openly question the morality of current corporate–managerialist policies and practices – morality in the sense of 'the active search for individual worth' (Hodgkinson, 1991, p. 130) and/or the sense of 'making a difference' (Fullan, 1993, p. 80).

Recently, in research and consultancies in a number of public-sector organisations, the author has witnessed managers agonising over the ethics of their management practices, and on the absence of meaning and purpose in their work lives. Increasingly, they question the deeper purpose or meaning of their actions in the light of such values as trust and honesty in relationships, and social conscience and justice in their dealings. Many refer to this as thinking about the 'spiritual' aspects of their work. I interpret this concern for spirituality as at least partly an attempt to understand the 'connectedness' of their work, their relationships, indeed their lives, to something beyond self, and to something that demonstrates to them that they do, in fact, make a difference.

Unfortunately, the reality in many organisations is that truth, honesty, and spiritual connections are the exception (Duignan &

Bhindi, 1997). Too many believe that the path to success needs to be camouflaged in untruth, even deception. Some managers wear a mask of authenticity, a façade of respectability, rarely revealing their true selves. Some are so used to their dramaturgical performance that they would hardly recognise their 'true selves'. Some educational leaders, in fact, may be tempted to allow their perceived role to submerge their 'self' and work hard to project a rarefied version of themselves. Some leaders are prone to 'image manipulation' as they present 'dramaturgical performances' instead of 'authentic and substantive administrative work' (Hodgkinson, 1991, p. 59). Hodgkinson concluded, somewhat negatively but perhaps realistically, that there is no *prima facie* ground for assuming that leaders are honourable men and women and that it may be safer to treat all leaders as suspect until proven otherwise. He argued that the problem of *leader character* has to be regarded as fundamental to any study of leadership (Hodgkinson, 1991, p. 60).

There is a gleam of hope, however. In recent times, the demands for increased efficiency and vertical accountability within an economic rationalist framework are being increasingly balanced by concerns that all these corporate–managerialist imperatives should be counterbalanced by commitment to ethical, moral and authentic leadership principles and practices (Duignan *et al.* 2003). This development, from my point of view, is very pleasing.

A call for ethical, authentic leadership

Leaders are increasingly expected to comply with ethical and moral standards in their relationships and practices (Fullan, 2003). Many educational leaders face increasingly demanding and discerning clientele who may challenge the reasons for decisions and the ethical foundations on which they are based. This can place pressure on leaders and cause them to adopt knee-jerk responses to confusing and ethically charged crises. Often leaders have no operational frameworks for dealing with such complex ethical issues.

There also seems to be a growing call, in the relevant literature, to reclaim the moral, ethical and spiritual domains of leadership (Bhindi & Duignan, 1997; Conger & Associates, 2004; Covey, 1992;

Duignan & Bhindi, 1997; Fullan, 2003; Handy, 1997; Sergiovanni, 1992 & 1999). Sergiovanni (1999, p. 22) has long championed the idea that leadership and administration are essentially moral activities. He has advocated the need for educational leaders to bring together head, heart, and hand in practice because leadership is, essentially, 'a moral craft'. Fullan (1993 & 2003) too, has strongly promoted the idea that both teaching and educational leadership must have moral purpose.

In 1993, he argued that the key building block for education as a moral enterprise '. . . is the moral purpose of the *individual* teacher' (p. 10). In 2003, he claimed that 'moral purpose of the highest order' provided the environment where all students learn, the gap between high and low performance is minimised, and students go forth from their schools enabled as successful citizens 'in a morally based knowledge society' (p. 29). He argued that this will not be achieved without a 'deep cultural change that mobilizes the passion and commitment of teachers, parents, and others' (p. 41) to promote and support authentic learning experiences for the students.

In a passionate and insightful argument for ethical leadership in education and schools, Starratt (2004a, p. 8) argued that leadership involves 'the cultivation of virtues' that generate authentic approaches to leadership and to learning. His major message is that the true test of leadership is the degree to which it becomes moral. He also argued that educational leaders have to take responsibility for changing those things over which they have some control in order to 'promote the deeply human fulfilment of young people' (Starratt, 2004a, p. 144). He pointed out that moral leadership '. . . invites others to transform each day into something special, something wonderful, something unforgettable, something that enables their human spirit to soar and, giddy with the joy of the moment, know who they are' (p. 145).

A challenge seems to be, however, that the environmental issues and forces discussed so far in this chapter mean that educational leaders operate in a context that can be inimical to ethical and socially responsible leadership. They will need to be cognisant of this fact if they are to respond ethically and authentically to the challenges identified in chapter 2.

The discussion, analysis and recommendations in the remainder of this book attempt to take up part of Starratt's earlier challenge for educational leaders to transform each day into something special, something that enables their human spirit to soar. I attempt to challenge educational leaders to 'know more deeply who they are' so that they can confidently tackle the complex and multi-dimensional ethical challenges identified and discussed in chapters 2 and 3. These ethical dilemmas are derived from the findings of a three-year research study entitled 'Contemporary challenges and implications for leaders in frontline human service organisations' (Duignan *et al.* 2003).

The research study

A three-year research study, supported by the Federal Government in Australia (ARC Linkage Grant), was conducted by the author and a team of researchers from the Australian Catholic University (ACU) on the challenges facing contemporary leaders in service organisations. While the research was conducted in a variety of organisations, for example, the police service, health care and religious institutions as well as in education (both State and Catholic schools), the focus of this book is on educational organisations, especially schools, and on educational leaders.

The following questions formed the basis of the research:

1 What are the contemporary challenges for leaders in frontline human service organisations?
2 How are leaders responding to these challenges?
3 What are the ethical dilemmas and underlying values involved in making these responses?
4 How are these challenges impacting on contemporary leadership practice?
5 What are the implications of these findings for the preparation and professional development of leaders?

A combination of quantitative and qualitative data collection and analysis techniques was employed in a complementary fashion (Hede & Wear, 1993) in the study. The study incorporated four data collection stages: questionnaires, interviews, critical leadership incidents, and electronic dialogue on an interactive website.

Questionnaire

The questionnaire was developed to 'map' the research area. It was designed to explore the main dimensions of the research questions with a stratified sample of front-line, middle and senior/executive leaders. Of the 3000 questionnaires distributed through partner organisations (police, education, religious), 1260 were returned: a response rate of 42%. Of these, approximately 400 were received from educational leaders. The findings from the questionnaire were used both to identify key concepts related to the research questions and to help formulate the questions for the interviews.

Interview

Semi-structured interviews were conducted with a selection of leaders who had volunteered to be interviewed. Of the 105 interviews undertaken either face-to-face or by telephone, and subsequently transcribed, 40 were from educational leaders.

Critical Incident Technique (CIT)

Critical incidents capture some of the dynamics of leadership choices and dilemmas and are a 'catalyst for examining leadership processes' (Parry, 1998, p. 96). The 300 participants who indicated their willingness to complete a critical leadership incident report were asked to describe one incident where they, as leaders, were forced to make a difficult ethical choice. They were asked to briefly recount what happened, the dynamics and processes involved, the choices they made and the lessons learnt. These incidents inform most of the tensions discussed in chapter 3. Of the 155 critical incidents returned, 55 were from educational leaders.

Interactive website

A customised interactive website constituted an important data-gathering, concept-validation, and theory-building technique. The 535 respondents interested in participating were invited by letter and email to join a three-week, on-line research dialogue on leadership, especially on the challenges and ethical dilemmas they faced in their workplaces. This moderated website was designed to focus on 'discussion topics', which were identified from the findings of the questionnaire, critical incident technique, interviews and emerging data on the website.

Data analysis

Questionnaire data were analysed using a variety of quantitative analysis techniques. NVivo (Bazeley & Richards, 2000), a computer analysis software package for qualitative data, was used to help analyse the large volume of data generated by the interviews, critical incident technique, and interactive website. It proved to be a powerful integrating tool that greatly assisted in the generation of concepts and theoretical propositions from the data across the different organisations (police, religious and both State and Catholic education).

Data generated through the website were continually processed, analysed and presented back electronically to participants in the form of a dialogue on emerging themes and concepts. This iterative process helped ensure that the emerging concepts fitted with the real world, were relevant to the people involved in the research, and made sense across the range of organisational contexts.

From the analysis of both the quantitative and the qualitative data a number of key leadership challenges were identified. These are discussed in the following chapter.

Key ideas for reflection

Educational leaders live and work in a global world that shapes social processes and institutions and encourages forms of individualism that may contribute to more selfish modes of living, often eschewing ethical and moral considerations. The pursuit of intense individualism can lead to a disengaged approach to life and living, more self-centred and competitive choices, and practices that may be very destructive of collegial and collaborative relationships in schools and school communities.

In parallel with these developments, many schools have embraced corporate management practices, which are based on efficiency, standards, targets, productivity and accountability. These characteristics have tended to replace the professional dimensions of service, compassion and collegiality.

In addition, some schools continue to base their educational practices on traditional philosophies and paradigms, which, combined with the other developments, can create dependency, even addiction, in their students.

Ethical and moral standards need to be maintained in all forms of leadership. The idea that teaching and leadership must have ethical and moral purposes should be a key consideration for educational leaders, despite the fact that contemporary educational work environments tend not to support and nourish ethical and moral educational practices. Educational leaders need to challenge unethical and immoral policies and practices wherever they find them; especially the morality and validity of ingrained patterns of inequality in the delivery of educational services. Ethical and authentic action is essential.

Questions for reflection

- What global pressures are impacting on you as an educational leader and how are you responding to them?
- In what ways might schools and schooling contribute to the development of addictive life processes in their students?
- How can schools better prepare students to make choices that are oriented to their all-round development as human beings?
- How can schools better prepare students to choose a healthy life–work balance and a commitment to community values?
- How can schools specifically help students to develop ethical and moral frameworks for life and work?

Chapter 2

Key challenges for educational leaders

The challenges in this chapter and the tension situations in the next chapter are accompanied by explanatory or illustrative cases. Some of the details of these cases have been changed to help ensure anonymity without affecting their key messages.

Providing a values-driven vision

One of the distinguishing characteristics of successful educational leaders is their capacity to provide a vision for the future and inspire hope in those with whom they work. They also lift the spirits of their people and help them to translate the vision into the daily practices of their work. In this way they help to inject meaning into the daily grind of getting the work done, thereby providing a sense of purpose and direction.

The articulation of vision necessarily involves leaders sharing their hopes, desires and expectations with the members of the school community, and establishing the foundations of an organisational culture that supports the aspirations of all stakeholders. The intent and content of the vision helps motivate all the members of the school community. Reflection on, and communication of, this vision is essential if it is to become part of everyday practice.

Linking vision to practice seems to be a vital component in the relationship of the leader and those led. Drawing people beyond their daily tasks and routines and engaging them in helping to shape a desired future facilitates the creation of a more meaningful and inspiring workplace. The formative nature of this process also seems to be important in bringing people to a fuller understanding of their purpose and direction, and to a strategic sense of their work.

Educational leaders are challenged to engage with their staff in ways that take the whole group forward, rather than plugging gaps and responding primarily to perceived emergencies. It is wasteful of time, energy and talent to simply fill gaps as they appear, without reflecting on and working through what is really needed to position the school to meet future challenges. Communicating the strategic purpose to everyone is vital in drawing together staff at all levels. Clear purpose, inspirational communication, and an appeal to agreed values and belief systems, will point clearly to the road forward.

A major problem identified by a number of leaders in the study was finding the time to reflect on and communicate a vision in the face of busy schedules. A principal of a school summed up this issue very well: 'I see a very important part of the leadership role as having time to reflect on direction, to have a sense of vision and to lead others who share that vision, but I find that a great challenge to that is finding the time within the daily routines to ensure that you structure that in'.

Leaders cannot do it all by themselves. They have to work with and through others to achieve their organisation's vision and goals. There is simply not enough time in the workday for one person to provide the scope and depth of leadership required in contemporary school communities. A principal encapsulated it when he said that, 'You have got to be a strong communicator and relationship builder. You have got to have the capacity to build relationships, to make connections, to build partnerships, to build strong alliances with others'.

The principal is referring here mainly to relationships internal to the organisation but of course leaders also have to develop and maintain strong external relationships and networks. They have to be effective public advocates and they need to represent the organisation in various public arenas. This is especially important in an era when education is seen to be everyone's business and is continually under scrutiny and critique by a sometimes sceptical public.

It is too much to expect that one person, the designated leader, can meet all these expectations satisfactorily. Leadership can no longer be regarded as the property, even the monopoly, of one person: the principal. Emerging wisdom on leadership suggests that there needs to be greater sharing and distribution of leadership responsibilities in educational organisations (Crowther *et al.* 2002b). The need to develop effective relationships and engage others in leadership in the school context is obvious. Sharing leadership with others is both necessary and wise, and is discussed in chapter 7 in this book.

However, achieving a dynamic balance between coping with current realities and keeping a strategic eye on the future is difficult for most educational leaders. A principal suggested that one way to help maintain this balance is to involve key stakeholders in generating a strategic vision while, at the same time, ensuring that day-to-day concerns are not neglected.

Many of the educational leaders in this study pointed out that having a set of core values was critical to the leadership role of setting vision and direction. These values, they argued, need to be clearly articulated and communicated as a basis for organisational purpose and direction. There is no better way of serving this purpose than by communicating directly with organisational members so that they are aware of the nature of their psychological contract as members of that organisation. The legal contract of employment, of course, is only one aspect of the contract necessary to become and remain an effective member. Active membership requires engagement at a deeper, affective level where there is a close relationship between personal and organisational values.

Knowing the values that motivate organisational members and articulating these values clearly can assist in developing a shared vision and mission for the school. Clarity of purpose based on a shared set of values and expectations would seem to be fundamental to effective educational leadership.

Managing staff relationships

A dominant theme in leadership is that it must be relational, that is, by definition effective relationships are the energy source of leadership. A principal stated that valuing others is the key to the development of authentic relationships:

> The promotion of staff morale, keeping staff motivated, cultivating teamwork and providing opportunities for staff development are some of the greatest challenges for leaders of educational organisations. It could be said that valuing others is a common thread in these elements and provides an authentic bond between the leader and those in the group.

Empowering others, delegating authority and simply trusting people to get on with their tasks should underpin leader–staff relationships in ways that link strategic purpose to everyday practices. However, usually when trust is breached there is a tendency to retreat to the classical organisational model, with remote personal exchanges, reliance on quasi-legal rules, and withdrawal to a hierarchical and bureaucratic form of control. A principal of a school commented on what happens when trust is betrayed:

> What happens to the leadership relationship when there is a massive breach of trust? This is not an uncommon occurrence. The leader retreats to a position of power and control. The aggrieved staff members feel excluded and do not give of their best. Morale is affected adversely.

Some leaders believe that developing relationships requires too much time and resources. This is an inappropriate way to think about relationship-building. Developing relationships for their own sake, or conversely for instrumental purposes, is not what authentic leaders do. They regard relationship-building as one of the core ways that value-driven organisations value all those who work in and for the organisation. It is the way a school, as a community, actively and fully engages its talented key stakeholders, giving them a sense of belonging and encouraging and supporting their commitment to the purposes of the organisation. Building relationships is not just a matter of managing the people in the organisation but of providing the leadership necessary to marshal the most valuable resources, the people.

Leading people

Many educational leaders find it a challenge to determine how 'relational' relationship building should be. Those who have been apprenticed in a hierarchical, control-type model of leadership are often unsure of how close relationships should be, especially with those who are accountable to them. It is important to distinguish here between personal and professional relationships in an organisation. Professional relationships must, of course, have a personal dimension, but it is equally important to develop personal relationships within a professional framework. The issue is not how friendly formal leaders should be with those who work with them, but how all organisational members can work closely and professionally together to achieve the goals and objectives of the organisation. Professional relationships must always be predicated on the core values espoused in the organisation. Being honest, trusting and trustworthy, respectful, tolerant, empathetic, open to critique, and willing to be a team person are as essential to professional relationships as they are to the development and maintenance of personal relationships.

In a school setting, core values also include valuing students and the educational processes that best serve their needs. The bottom line in a school community setting is how well relationships serve the needs of students and their parents.

Often, however, educational leaders face the problem of dealing with poor performance and balancing their professional responsibility for ensuring the smooth operation of their organisation with their personal feelings for those staff who are not performing adequately. Time and again the practical difficulties related to this issue were noted in interviews in the study. A typical example was provided by a school principal:

> My clerical assistant has been very unprofessional and, at times, rude and unhelpful to all of her colleagues. I have had interviews with her regarding her attitude and interpersonal skills. The incidents are repeated almost daily and occur in the workplace. They impinge upon others' personal lives as well.

Many educational leaders find it difficult to face up to finding a resolution to such problems. They prefer to think that if they ignore the situation it will go away. Some such challenges are potentially very serious issues and are often the source of much concern and stress for leaders. A principal of a school described a tension-filled event that he found very difficult to manage:

> I can give you an example of one [tension] that we've just had recently which is: we've got a young boy here who has been here for three years and he's diagnosed as having [medical] problems and is on medication and he is a big lad and his home life isn't so wonderful. He takes out his aggression here at school. What happened last year is that we had another lad here who is physically handicapped and for whatever reason this other boy decided that he wanted to attack him and he did, he actually kicked him and bruised him. The parents of the injured boy were very upset but they were prepared to forgive.
>
> The staff here thought that this was an outrage and regardless of the parents they wanted the boy [who'd attacked the other] removed. It was an interesting situation, in that the dilemma I had was all about: where does this boy go if we remove him from the school? The parents were forgiving and understanding and were prepared to just set up structures so it wouldn't happen again and also to guarantee that this boy would never go near their son again. That was a major tension because it took a little while to realise that we couldn't guarantee to this other family that we could be everywhere all the time with this boy to guarantee it . . . . what it meant for me was an awful lot of sleepless nights worrying about all the different avenues.

These issues are illustrative of the range and difficulty of the challenges involved when dealing with tension situations involving leading people in educational organisations. Educational leaders often avoid confronting such problems if they can, because they believe that solutions are hard to find and the legal environment of the employment contract often ensures that the poor performer or difficult person will not be dealt with promptly, if ever. So a response often is: 'Why put yourself in an unwinnable position that may also undermine your future effectiveness as a leader?'

Balancing personal and professional responsibilities

Maintaining a proper balance between personal needs and professional responsibilities is problematic for many educational leaders. In attempting to maintain a balance between personal and professional responsibilities, as well as coping with the pressure of heavy workloads, educational leaders speak of feeling 'inundated' and of having to do more and more without sufficient support.

Resource pressures in educational organisations are contributing significantly to this problem. 'Inundation' implies that educational leaders are generally overwhelmed by the pressures to achieve the same or greater outcomes with fewer resources. The impact of technology is no doubt promoted as improving the input–output ratio of the flow of work processes. However, electronic technology may be contributing to the feeling of inundation. The implication is that many leaders feel that they are being thrown 'off balance' or 'out of balance', with their work lives dominating their personal and private lives.

The demand for more efficient use of time and resources results in some of those resources being drawn from the personal or private sources of these leaders. They find that their personal time, especially, is encroached upon to an unacceptable level. This imposition on private time, that has traditionally been a feature of the private sector, is now more and more characteristic of leadership in the public sector.

Many educational leaders perceive that more advanced technology is not redressing the balance. A principal put it quite succinctly:

> . . . we are doing an awful lot, with a lot less. Our time is really precious, we are inundated not just at my level . . . but all levels of the organisation . . . we are inundated by this technology which is supposed to be so helpful.

The following extract from an interview with a school principal indicates the heavy time demands of the job and the added pressures coming from the use of communication technology, especially ubiquitous emails. He states:

> Well, it's pretty much a seven-day working week. I think I'm usually in the office for about 9 or 10 hours [each day]. When I get home at night I might do a bit of reading but I'm not the sort of person who goes home and gets back on the computer. On the weekend I would. All of us e-mail each other about this, that and the other on Sundays and it is becoming an expectation.

> *Question*: Is it becoming a game?

> *Response*: Yes, I think so. One of the standing jokes is about how late the e-mails get sent and about how you can set your computer to send e-mails at 2.02 am. You can get e-mails being sent at 9 or 10 pm . . . I get e-mails from my boss at 5.30 am. Of course, what I think it has done is increase the pressure enormously. Initially, it sounds like a really good and efficient time-saver. You don't have to worry about long telephone conversations when you do relationship building, you can just dash off this e-mail but it has compressed the time frame, so instead of having more time the benchmark's gone up so you are supposed to deliver more work.

This principal is really describing a power game being played. There would appear to be a lack of thought, even respect, for the person on the receiving end of the email messages; the implication being that the person is at the beck and call of the one in control, the one with the greater organisational power. Time for reflection and mature consideration for problem-solving purposes is clearly limited by the pressures to respond quickly to emails, to be seen to be 'on the ball', as it were.

There is also a tension or inner conflict for some leaders as they wrestle with the conflicts between personal and organisational goals. This conflict can eventually lead them to question whether the commitment to remain with the organisation is worth the personal sacrifice. The question of continuing to commit can consume the person's thoughts about his/her role in the organisation. If work and relationships within the organisation no longer inject meaning into daily life, then quitting, or at least disengaging, becomes a possibility. A principal stated:

> I must say that, at times, I can become quite philosophically disengaged because I think it is not . . . an organisation that I came into and was committed to . . . So, I have, at times, felt that my overall personal challenge was to maintain my engagement and maintain my commitment . . . and get on with it, as opposed to saying 'I don't think I can work in this organisation,' or, 'I don't believe the policy framework is going to be suited to my philosophical, educational background'. So that sort of sums up the issues that I am facing at the moment.

The element that seems to be absent here is the identification of methodologies or processes to systematically determine priorities. Clear priorities could alleviate the stress and conflict that arise when pressures become too great for the individual to withstand. This challenge was identified by a principal as part of the daily tasks that must be met as part of the balancing act:

> Just on a day-to-day level the biggest challenge is dealing with the competing priorities and the volume of work and the volume of issues you've got to stay on top of, professionally and managerially.

However, few educational leaders seem to have developed specific strategies and methodologies for dealing with the complexity of their jobs, for establishing priorities in their work, or for targeting specific professional development to assist them. Educational leaders, also, did not seem to use the job or the workplace as a basis for experiential growth and learning. In fact, the opposite seems to be more the case: the job and the workplace are seen to be inimical to personal and professional learning and growth.

It would appear that the feeling of being inundated and overwhelmed by the job causes many educational leaders to withdraw within themselves, to become defensive, and to rely more on formal methods of communication (e.g. email or memos). Instead of building relationships, such communication habits can inhibit relationship development.

Communicating effectively

Good communication requires, first, that one has something important to communicate, second, that one chooses appropriate times and means to deliver the message, and third, that one actively engages with others beyond a simple one-way communication to clarify the intended message and dispel misunderstandings. Meaningful engagement and dialogue with staff in their day-to-day working lives facilitates effective communication.

Large systems are sometimes slow to process issues and problems, so gaps in communication may occur between those who make the decisions and those who implement them. Leaders may assume that everyone in the organisation knows where they are going and why, but these are not safe assumptions. Many staff in organisations are heard to say: 'Why doesn't anyone tell me anything around here?' or, 'Why am I the last to know what is happening around here?'

No matter how much communication is used, no matter how accessible it is, down the line or at the local level, messages will be subject to different interpretations. One of the responsibilities that leaders have is to correct misinterpretations and put to rest certain myths. Without this, sometimes the myths develop a life of their own and a rumour can become accepted as fact.

There is no guaranteed process for ensuring that people in an organisation are optimally informed about new policies and changes. Often people will hear what they want to hear and reject or distort what they perceive not to be in their interests. The size of the organisation, of course, influences the degree to which formal leaders can engage in one-to-one conversations, which are the most effective form of communication.

The CEO of a large bank in Australia made an art form of communicating regularly through videos, especially on key topic areas or current issues, with all staff members. Staff generally appreciated his attempt to personalise his communication. No matter how large the school community, principals particularly must devise creative ways of engaging directly with key stakeholders. Every means, formal and informal, must be used to keep all stakeholders informed and up-to-date. If nature abhors a vacuum, then so do organisations: if communication isn't regular and meaningful, then someone (or some group) will invent a version of events, and rumours will spread to fill the void. This is especially true when leaders are attempting to bring about change in their organisations. Change usually threatens some organisational stakeholders and fears can be exacerbated if the facts of the change are distorted or manipulated by those who are resistant to the change.

If, as an educational leader, one is clear about one's core values and vision for the organisation, and also understands how these values and vision can inspire others, communication is likely to flow much more easily. If the leader's own personal values are explicit and well understood by key stakeholders this will assist them to interpret communications 'in the right spirit' on first reading or listening. Effective educational leaders have the capacity to use both formal and informal communication to build relationships, partnerships, and strong alliances.

Leading continuous change

We live in times of rapid change and transition. In such periods, it is necessary to realise that there may be casualties in any change process. Part of leadership is recognising that not everyone is going to come on board immediately, or even in the short-term, with new ways of thinking and doing. Leaders need to be sensitive to the fears and anxieties of those involved in a change process. As one principal wisely suggested, 'You have to have a set plan on how you are going to deal with that [change]. You have to be caring and have a plan that maintains their self-esteem. You cannot dump people. I think that is an important aspect of leadership'.

One principal, when attempting to introduce a mechanised system of reporting, found that the change better reflected the school's value system but that this was not necessarily appreciated by a number of staff members. She learned that during the process some staff feared that they would not be able to cope with the new system of reporting. The principal used different approaches, including one-to-one discussions and public announcements, to help allay these fears but to also make it clear that the change would happen and that it was in their interests to be part of it.

As leaders, we may, in fact, perceive others to be overreacting to change when they seem to be reacting more than we are (Bridges, 1995, p. 22). Leaders of change need to remind themselves that 'changes cause transitions, which cause losses – and it's the losses, not the changes, that they're reacting to' and that 'it's a piece of *their* world that is being lost, not ours' (p. 22, italics in original).

Leaders who are trying to manage a top-down change may be reluctant, according to Bridges, to talk openly about the change, '. . . arguing that it will "stir up trouble" to acknowledge people's feelings' (p. 23). But leaders of change *must* engage openly with those who will be affected by the change, and they must acknowledge and address positively the losses and psychological transitions being experienced by these people. Research about what helps people recover from loss concludes that 'they recover more quickly if the losses can be openly discussed' (Bridges, 1995, pp. 23–24).

One way to help overcome fear of loss in change situations is for leaders to devise change strategies that strike a balance between top-down and bottom-up change. Those affected by the change must not only be consulted about the change but also actively engaged in its genesis. A principal cautioned that:

> The processes used for the implementation of change can, as a matter of course, alienate members. This is especially true if the change and the change processes are mandated from the top down without adequate, if any, consultation with those who are most affected by the change.

Most people do, of course, have the capacity to change; it is a part of life and this capacity for change is inherent in us all. Those affected by change need to know that the comfort zone they leave will not be replaced by a situation that creates unnecessary conflict and tension for them. Some who initially resist change may finally become excited by it and transformed when given the opportunity to experience the change in a practical situation, especially if they are encouraged and supported by those in leadership positions. A principal emphasised the need for a supportive leadership approach that is sensitive to the level of readiness of those who are expected to change and/or to implement change:

You have got to be there for them when that [change resistance] happens. Yes you know how they feel and you can say '*God I feel the same way*' and, in fact, there is a lot of commonality to be shared. People want to know that you appreciate where they are; if they are not ready for this they may be ready in six months' time.

Some meet the challenge of change by accepting the need to be up-to-date and involved through professional associations and networks with other members of staff across the organisation and the wider educational community. Networking outside one's organisation is one way to break out of group thinking and be exposed to national and international thinking. This means taking time to reflect on professional literature, since change can often be predicted, because it is happening in other countries. Networking can be an accelerator of change because it is reassuring to share with colleagues who are struggling with the same issues and coming to similar conclusions. Also, as one principal stated, 'on a personal level, it is good to have kindred spirits.'

The challenge to lead in a time of change is a difficult one, because it often requires a shift from a hierarchical world model to an inclusive, transformational leadership model. Some educational leaders in this study acknowledged that they still used a control model more than an inclusive model because they have not shifted their mindset to the new paradigm in which they now live. The new paradigm has different assumptions and a different context from the old paradigm within which many leaders were trained and developed. An educational leader in the study summed it up well:

The old, put simply, is born of mechanism and clocks and enlightenment and the new is born of complex living systems. Once you appreciate how that works you work from a different metaphor and often the metaphors carry more significance than the facts. Once you work from a different metaphor it is more difficult, but I have a sense that, in terms of making decisions for the future, you'll actually be more in tune with what's [likely to happen] in the future. Today will be a preparation for the future, to get the right direction, but what we tend to do is go back to the old framework to make our decision because we are more comfortable there and more secure and we can often put a better argument. It's the whole cult of rationalism we get caught in, whereas in the new [paradigm] it's much more to do with the whole and the whole person, the creative imagination.

Some stakeholders are willing to be engaged in a process that is unfolding, and accept that change is automatically built into organisational life, because there has to be constant reviewing and making of key decisions that are part of the new way of looking at reality. How change is actually introduced can also have an important bearing on how such new ideas and new ways of thinking are accepted.

Frequently, principals in the study pointed to the poor performance of teachers as a special challenge when attempting to lead a change process. They suggested that the new accountability processes were bringing a cultural change to their schools.

Managing accountability and individual performance

The high public pressure for accountability in schools, in terms of definite outcomes, means that there is constant pressure to improve performance outcomes. The economic rationalist philosophy and managerialist practices that have influenced governments since the mid-1980s are now driving many educational organisations.

Many in the education sector see this managerialist approach as dominated by an expectation of 'doing more with less'. A principal claimed that these new management expectations have led directly to a change in culture in schools from a former collegial approach to one that is less open and collaborative:

> I think [there is a] complete change in culture and the way in which the organisation now operates. It's quite different from what we experienced [in the past], for example, it used to be a much more open and collaborative style but it has become quite different to that now. So that there is much less openness, much less collaboration.

Both scarcity of and constraints on resources are apparent in most educational organisations. However, it is not always clear whether this is driven by increased expectations of what can be achieved or by constant cuts in the resources available. Whatever the case, contemporary leaders perceive themselves as having to juggle their strategic objectives against insufficient resources.

It appears that a balance needs to be struck between 'hard' and 'soft' approaches to leadership so that individuals accept their accountabilities without feeling overwhelmed or directionless in a complex organisation. A balance between personal responsibility and teamwork is desirable, where the burdens are shared to make them more bearable. Also, there is a need to develop a more formative and developmental approach to accountability; current approaches often appear summative and punitive. Accountability processes must be just and equitable and should clearly reflect the core values espoused by the organisation. Where values are ignored or violated, accountability processes will be seen to be, and most likely will be, antithetical to the real purposes of an educational organisation.

Dealing with poor performance

The issue of dealing with poor performance in a responsible and professional manner that considers the interests of all concerned emerged as one of the most serious accountability challenges for educational leaders. Many leaders feel frustrated by supervisors' reluctance to deal with poor performance, often due to the perceived difficulty of the legal and industrial issues involved. For example, a principal considered it virtually impossible to improve the performance of poorly performing teachers, because, in his view, the union mostly supports the teacher without seeking to find out the facts.

While governments and education departments often take a strong line on this issue in the media, it is the principal who usually has to deal with the direct tensions and trauma involved. Apart from the uncertainty of knowing if they have made good decisions, principals have the stress of dealing with the emotional issues as well as the facts of each situation. A principal provided an insightful example of the difficulties and complexity surrounding many performance issues:

> At our school we have a teacher in his early fifties who has difficulty with consistency, leading to poor classroom management structures with some children in his class every year. The teacher is a nice person, well-liked by his peers. Most of the children in his class continue to perform at a reasonable level. However, this year three boys regularly disrupt the class. One of these boys, an extremely difficult child, is a challenge for any teacher.

The teacher in this example had taught at the school for over twenty years and during that time many staff worked with him to help with preparation and management strategies, however, similar problems seemed to appear nearly every year. The stress affected the teacher's wellbeing but he could not see any alternatives to teaching.

The principal in this situation had not instigated formal procedures because he regarded teaching as a caring occupation and the role of educational leader as one of helping and supporting people in a difficult profession where it is almost impossible to influence all thirty children in a class to the same level. The principal stressed that dealing with poor-performing staff is not as clear-cut as is often portrayed by the media or by political leaders.

The following example further illustrates this challenge for principals. A principal of a small K–12 school appointed a new teacher, about 50 years old, who had already converted a nursing degree into a qualification to teach biology and health education. In a very short space of time it became obvious, however, that she was going to struggle to get teacher registration. The principal had to decide whether to look after the teacher's personal welfare and provide her with far more support than would be normal, knowing that the educational outcomes for her students could be disastrous.

Eventually, district office personnel were alerted to the problem and accepted a recommendation that the teacher's probation be extended and that she be moved to another, larger, school with more resources to assist her. Mostly, the principal suggested that this was not a very satisfactory solution to such a problem; in fact, it merely shifted the problem sideways.

On reflecting on this experience, the principal pointed out that the first responsibility for an educational leader is to ensure the best possible outcomes for the students and suggested that in future he would:

> 'Bite the bullet': tackle the performance issue head-on and early. Any personal issues arising from this course of action will need to be dealt with, but I can no longer support or overlook inefficient teaching practices because of personal problems.

It is likely that a failure to act quickly and appropriately may damage the individual teacher, the students, or both, as in the case reported by the principal of a probationary teacher whose substandard performance led to complaints from students and parents. This teacher, who had also retrained from a previous career, grabbed or hit students on two occasions. Although he had been on a program of improvement, he showed little sign of progress and the principal did not believe he would ever achieve an acceptable level of performance. The principal, however, had concerns about the teacher's mental state, and had to weigh up this concern for the welfare of the teacher with his potentially disastrous impact on the students. The principal felt that he had no real choice, and decided to protect the welfare of the students by advising the teacher to seek an alternative career, or else he would initiate formal proceedings for dismissal. The teacher appreciated the principal's concern for the students, revealing that he had similar concerns himself, and resigned his position.

Another example is of a principal who had made the decision to dismiss a teacher who had been placed on a support and development program that had extended over two years. The teacher's ability to interact appropriately and effectively with staff was an issue. The principal involved the industrial relations personnel, a supervisor at the school, the teacher concerned, and a support person for the teacher, as well as the union. The principal considered that not only was there no evidence to indicate that the teacher was able to complete the required tasks, but also that any further assistance would require the input of huge resources from other staff, which would impact on their workload and stress levels, without an appreciable outcome. In reflecting on the incident, the principal concluded that, in spite of what policies state, when you are dealing with human beings, you are dealing with complexity. He decided that one must be pragmatic but must usually act for the good of the many.

The majority opinion of educational leaders in this study was that teachers' performance problems can and should be identified by leaders early in the teachers' careers. Support and a program of development should be given to those so identified. If a teacher shows no evidence of improvement as a result of such development opportunities, then those in leadership positions must protect the children under their care and set in train processes for the teacher to resign or be dismissed.

Leading an ageing workforce

The workforce in education is ageing. In many Western countries, the average age of teachers is in excess of 45 years (Santiago, 2001). Educational leaders in this research project considered it essential to professionally challenge people who have stagnated in the same role for years. A principal observed that it is rare to meet a person who has not become complacent after a number of years, unless he/she has had a change of responsibility. She suggested that it was difficult to find a person who could maintain enthusiasm over the long haul: 'I don't think any of us can afford in an organisation, like a huge educational institution as we are, to settle into anything.'

A challenge for any individual school and for a system of schools is to encourage an ageing teacher population to continue to meet the contemporary challenges of teaching and learning. Early retirement may lead to a great loss of organisational memory, wisdom and know-how; losses that could not easily be replaced even if financial resources were more plentiful. Some educators merely tolerate change while they serve their last few years. Such a response is especially serious at both teacher and leadership levels where it is essential to respond to change if the school is going to grow and prosper. There is a great danger that teachers and other educational leaders who are nearing the end of their careers will act as one principal suggested:

There are people who have reached pretty well the end of their careers or have gone as far as they want to go, who are satisfied to sit on their hands.

As the average age of educators continues to rise, education systems and schools need to devote more resources and generate creative solutions to ensure that teachers and other educational leaders continue to be professionally challenged.

Teachers with many years' experience should be more intimately involved in leadership and decision-making at their schools, a challenge that is discussed in greater depth in chapter 8. Formal leaders need to tap into their talents and expertise and challenge them to continue making a contribution to the core activities of their school. There is a need to celebrate the wisdom of experience and recognise and reward those professional teachers who are in the twilight of their careers. They should be encouraged and supported to 'share their wisdom' on teaching and learning, and to engage with younger teachers in a two-way dialogue on how to enrich the learning experiences of students in the school. A major challenge for school principals and other formal educational leaders in schools is to help build a culture of sharing and open dialogue on what really matters in schools – improving learning and teaching.

In an era when more and more professionals are searching for a healthier life–work balance many are opting for part-time employment or retirement, when they can afford it. There is a need for '. . . a variety of options for flexible work solutions to help keep life and work in balance' (Birch & Paul, 2003, p. 68). Such options could include: part-time employment; flexible working hours; shorter working hours; job sharing; and other family-friendly practices. Those responsible for policy and leadership in educational systems and schools must wake up to the reality of an ageing workforce.

It would appear, however, that much more is said than done about these challenges. Some will be difficult to resolve, but more leaders and organisations need to 'face up to the evident facts of the workplace' and dramatically change their ways of thinking and acting about these challenges (Birch & Paul, 2003, p. 80).

The discussion on leadership challenges in this chapter indicates that contemporary educational leaders face complex and varied challenges in their daily work. Within the areas just discussed, many of the challenges can be classified as tensions or dilemmas and these are the focus of the next chapter.

Key ideas for reflection

Educational leaders need to collaboratively develop and communicate a value-driven vision for the future in order to give a sense of purpose, meaning and hope to their school community. This envisioning process requires them to engage meaningfully with people, building authentic relationships in order to serve the needs of students and their parents.

A major challenge for educational leaders is to translate the vision into everyday practices. A good start is to create more purposeful and inspiring workplaces built on trust, transparency and open communications. While modern technology can be of great assistance in facilitating communication processes, the current dominance of emails can be impersonal and unrealistic in terms of their time-response expectations and/or their perceived urgency. Pressures of time and of continuous change may cause some educational leaders to disengage, withdraw into themselves, become defensive, or revert to formal methods of communication.

A major contemporary challenge for educational leaders is to lead people who are experiencing fear and psychological loss in a context of rapid and continuous change. They must engage openly with them to help them cope with their fears and anxieties. Top-down mandated changes especially can create great consternation and fear among those who have to implement them. Leaders need to be sensitive to the levels of readiness of those involved. Leading in conditions of continuous change requires a shift from hierarchical approaches to more inclusive transformational models that deal with the whole person.

One of the most demanding challenges for educational leaders is dealing with poorly performing teachers where there is deep concern for students under their care. Such situations are complex and multidimensional; however, the consensus seems to be that it is better for the principal to 'bite the bullet' and deal with the problem early and head-on.

Educational leaders in the twenty-first century need to devise new and creative ways of ensuring that teachers and other educators with many years of experience are continuously challenged and actively engaged in their own personal and professional development. Many with long years of experience can become stale and complacent if they are not constantly encouraged and supported to be reflective and creative practitioners.

Questions for reflection

- What strategies and processes do you use to develop a collaborative vision and then translate the vision into everyday practices?
- What strategies do you use to help ensure that you communicate meaningfully and authentically with teachers, students and other key stakeholders in your school community?
- What leadership style or approach(es) do you use when leading change in your school community?
- What are some of the most difficult challenges you have encountered when dealing with poorly performing teachers? How did you overcome these challenges? After reading this chapter, how might you deal differently with them in future?
- In what ways do you, as a leader, try to ensure that teachers are personally and professionally engaged and committed?

Chapter 3

Leadership challenges as tensions

Many of the major challenges facing educational leaders involve leadership in situations where values and ethics are contested (Duignan & Collins, 2003). Some of these challenges constitute what Wildy *et al.* (2001) call 'contestable values dualities', or 'ethical dilemmas' (Dempster, 2001).

'Dilemma' usually indicates a difficult and challenging situation that, according to the *Concise Oxford dictionary* (1984, p. 268) 'leaves only a choice between equally unwelcome possibilities', and the example they provide is 'on the horns of the dilemma'. However, the majority of the challenges discussed in this chapter represent situations where there are more than two alternative possibilities; in fact most of the challenges are multidimensional in nature. In this book, the word 'tension' is preferred to 'dilemma' to describe these situations, because it denotes that relationships exist between a number of 'contestable values dualities' and that the different possible solutions for each situation will reflect how these relationships are balanced. This approach has profound implications for the ways in which educational leaders respond to difficult and challenging situations. A more complete explanation of why it is best to treat a difficult and challenging situation as a tension is discussed in chapter 4.

The 'real challenges' of educational leadership – the ones that keep educational leaders awake at night, cause them to take stress leave or retire before their time – are tensions between and among people, especially those based on philosophies, values, interests and preferences. While managerial issues such as strategic planning, resource allocation, or organising and scheduling educational processes and tasks demand the application of sound management processes, it soon becomes apparent that the devil is in the details of the relationship issues between and among the people involved. Rarely can issues involving complex human behaviour be reduced to, or resolved by, logical and linear management processes, no matter how systematic or thorough these may appear.

The key challenges for educational leaders, especially principals, identified from the data in this study, involved complex and often conflicting human relationships and interactions. Many of these tension situations involved issues related to student discipline and teacher competence or incompetence. The examples that follow provide a clearer picture as to why many leadership challenges can be regarded as tensions.

A principal recounted an incident about possible student involvement in drugs that typifies the complexity, multidimensionality and tensions involved in many leadership challenges in schools:

> ... there are the expectations of staff who don't generally, and didn't in this case, know the full details of what had gone on. You had enough information to have certain expectations of how students would be dealt with and there were a number of competing needs in that. One is that some parents felt that any girl in any kind of drug activity in the school was creating an unhealthy environment for the students and should be asked to leave. There were other parents who actually contacted us and said that they were familiar with these girls and felt that they deserved a second chance ... Some people thought the girls should be admitted back to the school. The girls were at different stages of their academic careers and the implications for some would have been far more serious than for others. So all of those things came into the decision-making. There were some competing values. Valuing the need to create a safe environment for the remainder of the student body; wanting to also deal with these girls justly and to enable them to move on from their mistake; protecting the interests of the parents and also creating an environment in which staff felt that there was still a level of discipline within the student body and that we weren't going to give the wrong messages about that.

On the surface, the resolution to an issue of students being involved in drugs might appear to be rather clear cut. After all, use of illegal drugs is against the law and is certainly against school rules. A clinical application of rules would leave little room for any consideration of personal issues or extenuating circumstances in deciding the fate of the students. Suspension, at the very least, or more likely expulsion, would be the expected outcome. Yet a close scrutiny of the case just presented demonstrates that expectations and perspectives may differ when the human elements of a dilemma or tension situation are considered. Usually in situations of human drama, *either/or* thinking that adopts a one-dimensional response will not encompass the complexity of such issues. *Both/and* responses are more likely to lead to satisfactory outcomes. A more detailed exposition of this particular perspective is presented in the next chapter on analysing tensions.

The key lessons that emerge from such complex responses can be regarded as examples that have wider implications. In fact, a number of categories of tensions consistently emerged from leaders' responses in this study, though they were manifested in a variety of ways. The development of these categories of tensions as well as the selection of examples for each tension was guided by the work of Kidder (1995). The following categories of tensions form the basis for discussion in the remainder of this chapter. Each heading that follows uses 'and' instead of 'versus' to emphasise that a *both/and* approach to its resolution is usually preferable to an *either/or* approach.

Common good and individual good

This was one of the most frequently discussed tensions. There is a constant tension between deciding whether to support decisions promoting the good of the group or the rights of the individual. Generally, the 'group' or the 'community' was perceived by educational leaders to be the wider student body and their parents; while individuals were usually teachers and/or students.

Often decisions favoured the group or community over the individual. Principals, for the most part, noted the need to provide for a student's welfare and safety as well as his/her educational outcomes.

However, in these examples, a principal's decision to suspend or expel a student was usually influenced by the perceived detrimental effects of student misbehaviour on the class or school community. While students were not expelled without serious consultation and with a number of attempts to deal with the problems they were having, one principal stated: 'I learnt as well a benchmark for when the price for individual "good" is too high in relation to the "good" of the whole group'.

There are times when the decision favours the individual over the community or group. In every case of a tension in this area, principals expressed concern and compassion for the welfare of the individual. In cases where principals refused to expel students, the choice not to expel was governed by concern for the student's welfare and the basic right of every child to receive an education.

In the case of ineffective staff, long and loyal service was acknowledged but usually was outweighed by the concern for the needs of the student body whose education was being impacted upon by their lack of teaching prowess. One principal decided that the task of removing a long serving and loyal teacher was too difficult and opted to 'wait it out'. This decision was, in hindsight, regretted and the principal concluded that the decision to move the teacher on should have been made earlier:

> I should have put her on an improvement program. Her students deserved better . . . Some staff considered my lack of action weak, as she was also undermining my decisions. I sat her out. She's retired. I should have acted earlier before it got to the stage that there was only one or two years to go before retirement. I have learnt that the process of looking at duty and obligations in ethical dilemmas is really important and I let down the people who are my first responsibility: the children.

Another principal decided that it was too difficult to fight an ineffective staff member who was applying for voluntary redundancy for the second time. He considered the opportunity cost of initiating and implementing a dismissal process and decided to spend his time in more productive ways. Whilst the principal, in this case, did not believe that this payout should be approved, he decided to avoid the tension and possible conflict involved in following a dismissal process:

> I would have preferred to terminate his services. In the end, I approved his voluntary redundancy. I weighed up the time and effort involved in trying to bring an unwilling and uncommitted staff member up to speed against the other priorities I had, together with the emerging initiatives and projects which were in the planning stage. I also thought very carefully about where my time would be better spent in terms of staff development, change management, redirecting the organisational culture and re-positioning the school for the future. I also know what it is like to prove incompetence in the area I work in. I believe I made the right choice.

Issues like the ones just described present difficult, complex challenges to educational leaders that require them to see and appreciate a number of possible resolutions. Often a decision has to be crafted that constitutes a 'best fit' resolution, given the specific circumstances of the case.

Another example, as highlighted by a principal, further illustrates the complexity and multidimensionality between an individual student's rights or interests and the pursuit of the common good:

> A student came to the school after a fairly troublesome time at another school. She was very bright and had a great deal to offer but her behaviour was extremely difficult and disruptive. Initially she settled in well although, at times, she was challenging to teachers and in particular to myself. She would stand up to me publicly and always seek to challenge me in front of other students. I accepted this because I thought that we would eventually make a difference in this young person's life . . . It was really between the individual and the common good. This young person's future could be determined by my decision to ask her to leave the school. She passionately wanted to stay. She wrote at least six letters begging me to let her stay and promising me that she would change.

What is the principal to do? How is he/she to strike a proper balance between concern for the individual and the protection of the group (the common good)? We will see that a number of the tension situations discussed in the remainder of this chapter help shed further light on the complexities of this and will help in the development of a framework for managing such tensions.

Care and rules

Educational leaders continually face challenges and decisions that involve tensions between a concern for either 'care' or 'rules'. Care encompasses compassion, looking at the individual circumstances and making a decision that puts care and concern for the individual above rules and policies. Rules or policies provide guidelines for leaders on how to make decisions. Some leaders, however, argue that, by complying with rules, they are also fulfilling their duty of care to the community and, therefore, do not recognise any real tensions in this area.

In schools there are instances where educational leaders feel that they must follow the 'letter of the law' to protect their own careers and reputations, but this approach can have dire consequences for some individuals. An example was where a teacher disciplined a student for breach of rules on a school camp and, in order to placate the parents, the teacher was disciplined. Staff, and indeed the principal, agreed that the teacher had an impeccable reputation and acted appropriately. Another teacher was falsely accused of sexually assaulting an infant student. The teacher was a valued member of staff and the accusation was found to be baseless. However, the strict procedures related to sexual assault were implemented and, as a result, the teacher suffered loss of reputation and trust from the community and system.

There were occasions when those faced with a tension situation used the rules, primarily, to determine the outcome. In such situations, consideration was usually given to the feelings of both parties. When rules were rigidly adhered to, leaders reported that they felt that they had no alternative but to follow them because the law demanded it. Examples from this study include:

1 a student with aggressive behaviour was suspended with allega-
tions of drug use at home. The principal noted that a detailed
record of all interactions and decisions was kept;
2 in two cases of sexual assault, both principals strictly followed
procedural guidelines; and
3 in two cases involving violent parents, principals adhered strictly
to system guidelines.

It is important to note that in these cases, principals consulted
widely with appropriate authorities. These included system personnel, welfare agencies, police and other members of staff. Where
students were suspended or expelled, the rules were followed
by principals in order to protect the body of students and it
was considered also to be in the best interests of the students
who were directly involved, i.e. that they would learn from the
discipline.

Some principals, however, tended to emphasise care over rules
where the decision guidelines were not mandatory. Rules were suspended when leaders considered that a care outcome was a 'better'
resolution of the tension. For example, a disadvantaged student was
disciplined and because of the type of penalty should have missed
out on a major sporting event. The senior executive 'overruled'
these rules and the student was allowed to compete. This was said
to be a once-in-a-lifetime experience for the student. Care for the
student was, obviously, the prime concern. The principal gave the
following account of the incident:

> Our school has a policy where, if a student has received more than
> one 'blue slip', that student is not allowed to participate in spe-
> cial activities such as excursions, visits or play sports until his/her
> behaviour has improved. If it is their [sic] first 'blue slip', the
> ban is for one week only. One student, who is a talented athlete,
> had reached eligibility to participate at regional level. The stu-
> dent had received no support from home and has been known
> to run in bare feet! One week prior to the athletic event he earned,
> fairly, his first 'blue slip'. Technically the full week was up the day
> after the carnival. The dilemma of allowing this child a chance at
> the carnival was taken to the Executive who decided he should
> participate.

The executive, in fact, judged that it was in the long-term interests of this student to be able to participate in an event at which he excelled, and which would, most likely, aid in promoting his self-concept and self-esteem. Of course, they were cognisant of the fact that they were setting a precedent and that other students and their parents could question the fairness of their decision, given that other students had been dealt with in the past 'by the rules'. These are the types of decisions faced by educational leaders every day. In the end, it often means making a judgement as to whether the benefits outweigh the possible negatives.

There was another interesting case where a principal disregarded regulations. The Principal felt that this was in the best interests of the child and that the end result proved his judgement to be correct. He concluded, however, that this would probably not be a course of action that he would repeat again as the risks were high and, with maturity and experience, he would handle the matter differently. This principal told a story of a situation containing a number of tensions and dilemmas. While it is a lengthy example, it is included here because it highlights the complex and multidimensional nature of typical challenges facing educational leaders on a daily basis. It especially highlights the difficult ethical choices faced by principals in the normal course of their work.

> The incident took place in a small town. This is the school of which I am principal. There was a child who attends the school; her mother who has a drug problem; and her grandfather who is a prominent citizen. The child's mother was neglecting the child involved as her lifestyle was not providing the child with the best opportunity for long-term success at school. As the grandfather lived in another town, my contact with him was limited to twice a year at face-to-face meetings, and fortnightly phone calls.
>
> There were a series of incidents involving the child that started to concern me. She was coming to school having no food, she was not being picked up in the afternoons, and her personal hygiene was being neglected. I contacted the Department of Community Services, as I am required to do, but nothing was done. I called the grandfather and told him about my concerns as well.

A week later, there was a fire at the child's house, due to the drugs that the child's mother had been taking. It could have been fatal. Later that week, the grandfather made a phone call to the school and asked to speak to the child. This is not in line with system policy, but I allowed the child to come to the phone. That afternoon she was taken from the local park by her grandfather and was sent to an aunt in another town. Two days later, the child's mother came to the school looking for her daughter.

This incident presented two ethical choices. The first was to allow the child to speak to her grandfather. This choice had to be made on the spot. I knew it was not within normal operating guidelines, but I felt it would be in the best interest of the child. I personally trusted the grandfather. This made the choice more difficult.

The second choice was after the child had been taken and her mother had come to ask if I knew where she was. I was prepared for this choice. I knew that it would come. I could tell her what had happened, tell her where her child was, or claim that I had no knowledge of the incident.

The choices I made were with the best interests of the child in mind. In the first instance with the phone call, I decided to allow the child to speak with her grandfather, knowing full well that I would be doing so outside the guidelines that were set down. When I was questioned by the child's mother as to her daughter's whereabouts, I decided to deny all knowledge of the incident while knowing that I should have reported it. The first choice was made for a number of reasons. I was becoming increasingly concerned for the child. I was actually relieved when I got the phone call and he asked to speak to his grandchild. I was hoping that it would result in an improved home situation for the young girl. The second choice, regarding what I would say if I was ever questioned regarding the child's removal, was an easier one, because I had time to think the situation through. I knew that other people in the town had seen the grandfather take the child and that it would only be a matter of time before she found out. I decided that no information that could lead to the child being returned to her mother would be coming from me. This decision was also formed partly due to my breach of guidelines in the first instance with the phone call.

With the benefit of hindsight, I'm not sure that I did make the right choices. The end result could not have been better. The child is now in a warm, safe environment and her mother's visits are short and supervised. No action was taken against anyone, and all parties are happy with the new situation. But I don't think that I can judge my actions purely on the basis of the final outcome. As a leader, I should have been able to work within the guidelines to bring about a favourable result. I think I showed inexperience. I was fortunate that the repercussions of my actions, and inactions, were positive. If I were faced with the same situation in the future, I would hope that I would handle the situation with a much greater sense of professionalism. In fact, I am confident that I would handle the situation differently.

This complex situation brings clearly into focus the tensions that can arise for leaders making decisions in situations where people's lives are involved. A rule approach to making decisions in such situations may appear to be the easy option but there is always the tug of the heartstrings pulling us toward a more caring and compassionate course of action. After all, teaching is a caring profession and educational leaders will always pay close attention to the needs of students as human beings.

In another example, a staff member was found to be inappropriately using system cars. The person in charge decided to waive the rules because she was informed that the 'accused' person was threatening to commit suicide. The leader concluded that while the rules had been waived in good faith, there was a sense of manipulation by the staff member. This leader also indicated that she would not adopt this approach in the future. She stated:

> It was reported to me that a person was suspected of inappropriately using a system car. My initial response was to take disciplinary action. The allegation was significant given that many thousands of kilometres were used privately. The situation arose as the person was fulfilling a role that was difficult to supervise.
>
> At the same time, I was contacted by a counsellor employed by the Employee Assistance Program stating that she believed the officer to be suicidal. I explained the misuse of the car to the counsellor. I was informed that his mental state was fragile.
>
> The ethical choice was whether to comply with system regulations concerning significant misuse or to avoid raising the issue to ensure

the welfare of this person. The choice became more difficult as I was also contacted by a number of principals who wished to raise other concerns about this same person.

I met with the person and had the staff welfare officer also in attendance. I highlighted the positive aspects of his work and let him know that his contribution was appreciated. I also let him know that his use of the car was sometimes not appropriate. I also informed him that I was not going to pursue the matter but wanted a commitment that he would comply with guidelines in the future. I did not raise the other issues as I considered they could be dealt with at a later stage. In this case, however, I considered the welfare issue to be more important than the misuse of resources.

In general terms, I believe the right choice was made, as it is my opinion that a leader has to place a high priority on the welfare of employees. Specifically, I am not sure, as subsequently I was informed that this person had threatened suicide on a number of occasions in different settings to have matters disregarded or to get his way.

What are leaders to do? They can never hope to know fully all the facts of any case or situation. They can only do the best they can with the information they can obtain by consulting those who may have information on the issue. Often, they have to follow their instincts as well.

These cases demonstrate that, in hindsight, leaders believed their care-based choices, while usually having positive outcomes for others involved in the situation, were not always the wisest courses of action for themselves. They seemed to have some regrets about taking the caring approach because doing so left them exposed to possible sanctions consequent upon breaking or bending the rules.

Long-term and short-term considerations

Any leadership decision has a range of possible long-term and short-term consequences. For example, a principal may decide not to expel a student, because, whilst it may bring short-term relief for the teachers who have to deal with this student, the decision may not be in the long-term interests of the student's education.

Leaders, if they are not reflective and strategic, can be over-whelmed by short-term pressures and perceived emergencies. In this way, they may be merely reacting to what they perceive as urgent, rather than to what is important, significant, and worthwhile. While it would be very unwise to neglect or ignore current realities, leaders must ensure that they remain strategic in their thinking and planning and stand apart so that they can bring a 'big-picture perspective' to any challenge or tension situation.

Another category of challenges faced by educational leaders reflect the tensions between the desire to be loyal to people, versus the need to be honest and see that justice is done.

Loyalty and honesty

Loyalty is defined as being committed to the organisation, the person in charge, or colleagues. Loyalty can constitute allegiance to individuals, groups or to the vision and mission of the organisation. Honesty is speaking truthfully about any person, issue or situation and refraining from intentionally deceiving or misleading.

A number of tensions involving loyalty versus honesty were identified by educational leaders in this study. The following examples provide insights into the nature of these types of tensions:

- balancing the recognition of long and loyal service against the need for restructuring and redundancies;
- making provision for older personnel to retire with dignity even though their current performance is not up to standard; and
- students balancing ethical issues related to their work for a teacher against their positive feelings and loyalty to the teacher.

An example of this last type of tension was provided by a principal. Students were asked by a teacher to enter the results of peers' marks into a computer:

> A teacher involved students in entering other students' results into the computer in preparation for writing reports. The incident took place in the teacher's office. She, the teacher, had asked to 'borrow' the students to assist her in preparing for some event. They had finished this work and were kept to do this report work. The teacher had told them to keep an eye out for any Faculty Leader and to

alert her if one came by. The students were not discomforted at the time. That evening one of them reflected with her father about the 'oddness' of the situation and how she felt uneasy. Her father suggested she come to see me, as principal. The students did so the next day and were very anxious that they would not be seen to be 'dobbing' but they felt they should not have been asked to participate in a clearly unethical activity.

In another incident, a principal faced a very personal quandary when dealing with an elderly teacher's classroom problems:

[An elderly member of staff] had been showing increasing signs of dementia for about two years. Several senior staff members expressed their concern but, more especially, for her students. I initially spoke with her husband whom I'd known for many years, thinking he would discreetly follow up the possible onset of dementia. My 'unwise' tactic resulted in her absolute denial of any problem. Nevertheless, I persuaded her to take long-service leave for a term. When she returned she was even more disoriented and students were becoming very distressed at her decreasing ability to teach. I was being deluged with complaints from staff, such as, 'When is she (me) going to do something about it?' and student complaints were naturally escalating . . . I chose the method of reduced teaching in the hope [the teacher] would eventually see that she was no longer able to teach . . . Her years of service precluded termination, and I knew she would not accept the offer of time out on sick leave . . . In the final analysis, the needs and rights of the students were the deciding factor in removing her from most of her teaching.

This is an example of a tension situation with numerous ethical dimensions. The tension between the values of loyalty and truth is very evident, but so also is the concern for the good of the individual and the need for the 'common good' to be protected, and the principal's care and compassion for the elderly teacher in competition with the need to follow rules and procedures on inadequate performance. Clearly, the tensions between these three 'contestable values dualities' make a complex tension situation that is best resolved by *both/and* thinking.

A tension that casts a wide shadow over many aspects of contemporary educational leadership is that of the recent emphasis on rationalist economic philosophies, strategies, and practices in leadership versus the need for a human service organisation, such as a school, to provide a 'human service'.

Service and economic rationalism

This tension highlights those instances where respondents believed that the imperatives of economic rationalism had a negative impact on their core business. Economic rationalism was considered to include making efficiency a core value, increased accountability and audits, use of redundancy to reduce costs, and restructuring (e.g. merging of organisational structures). The core business of schools, the *raison d'être* for their existence, in contrast, was considered to be providing a responsive, compassionate, high quality educational service.

Often in such situations, the emphasis by educational leaders was on 'maintaining the bottom line', or on meeting the imperatives of accountability. It appears, however, that the caring service dimensions of the tension are often implied, and are not always discussed directly when dealing with the situation. This is implied by the frequent acknowledgement that the increased emphasis on efficiency can have negative implications for the quality and level of educational services that can be provided by the school.

Several examples of these type of tensions were reported in the study. The following are examples from school principals:

- parents pleading questionable financial difficulties and wanting reduced fees, yet able to afford a new car;
- an organisation *driven* by performance and accountability with little consideration of the emotional impact on its culture and staff morale;
- funds allocated to those areas targeted as being high priority by the system, despite alternative priority requests from schools and teachers;
- funding required for students with special needs but resources being allocated, primarily, to improve academic outcomes; and
- rational economic corporate management demands clashing with individual leadership philosophies and styles.

A principal of a school gave an example, related to school fees, of a tension in this area:

> I think, most probably, one of the times when I do experience a little bit of tension is in making decisions when you have a parent in about school fees. For me sometimes this can be difficult. You really know that the parents are able to pay something, but they are really spinning you a great story about how they can't really afford to pay and you know that the person has just bought a new car, for example. There is also the justice issue because you know that out there is Mrs So and So, who is already a single parent and you've had several conversations with her and she is determined that she will pay the school fees in the best possible way she can.

Another principal commented on the problems that scarce resources, especially lack of staff, created:

> I think the other tension is to do with staff. It has been an enormously onerous task, and still is, for staff as we implement new assessment requirements. But most schools don't have the resources to make significant concessions in terms of time, and again that is a conflict in terms of caring for your staff and being driven by external requirements. That is an ongoing difficulty really.

Another area of tension recognised by principals in the study was that related to a corporate, hierarchical management approach to leadership in a collegial, collaborative educational context. One principal captured the essence of this tension:

> It [corporate culture] resembles a shift from, say, collaborative professionalism to a rational economic corporate management style. I think that's happening in a lot of organisations as people are consumed and absorbed by this sort of budget-driven approach to management.

Another principal explained the challenges imposed by decisions to reduce staff numbers and the tensions and human drama involved in responding to these challenges:

I had the job of handing out to two-thirds of the staff a big white envelope that said 'Would you like a voluntary redundancy? If you want to put your name forward this is what you'll get . . .' The impact on your support staff . . . is great . . . very difficult! Trying to keep the ship going and, at the same time, not always believing in these values. I'm the messenger, I've got to stand up in front of the staff and say that this is what we are doing and this is why we are doing it and, at the same time, not believing that it was the best thing in every aspect.

So that's very hard to do and it is very hard not to overlay your own perspective and undermine it. So this is difficult for me to get up and say that this is what our bosses have decided and then not say, 'Well, I think it stinks'.

He went on to say that passing on orders from 'on high' that he didn't personally agree with was very difficult for him. His belief in the integrity and worth of the individual made it difficult for him to give orders that treated individuals as expendable:

Conveying to staff the message from on high is not very palatable for me. My beliefs are in the individual. I think an educational organisation is based on teaching individuals and every person within it should be treasured and valued and cultivated and you just shouldn't be saying to people that we really don't need your sort any more. We should be saying, perhaps, 'your profile is not what we actually need but we can look around for another position for you, we can retrain you', but we've moved away from that to being a more typical private sector [organisation].

There was a strong view, however, among most principals in the study that, despite budget restrictions and economic imperatives, it is always possible to exercise care and concern for those with whom they work. A strong recommendation was the need to be fair in relationships and provide others with the reasons for why you decided the way you did. Honesty, it appears, is the best policy when trying to manage complex and tension-filled situations.

The leadership challenges identified by many leaders in this study included another category of tension that was usually described as 'status quo *versus* change and development'. These situations cover all those where various staff members disagree as to whether the 'way they currently do things' (status quo) is preferable to suggested new ways of thinking and doing (change and development).

Status quo and change and development

Maintaining the status quo is about avoiding and resisting change. Development or growth implies embracing changes. (A principal)

There were claims by a number of principals that many staff, especially those close to retirement, are marking time, and are content with doing things as they have always been done. A principal reported that:

A teacher, in the last years in the service, had been an outstanding practitioner but was now tired and cynical. His room looked like his attitude. All new policies were treated as, 'We've done this before, if you don't change it will go away'.

Another principal was cynical about the prospect of changing many of the older teachers:

When you look at the demographics of the teaching profession now, it's an ageing profession. There are fewer young people coming in, but yet there are more and more changes put in place. Many of the older members of staff are resistant to change. There is a cynicism; they've seen it all before, right through to the extreme of, 'I won't be here much longer, why put myself through this messy stage of change and learning new skills?'

It was suggested that many older personnel are choosing to retire rather than cope with rapid change. In some cases, the loss of the experience and knowledge of these older members of the organisation is perceived by leaders to be detrimental to the life and effectiveness of the school. When older members retire, vital organisational memory and wisdom can be lost with them.

It is unfair, however, to brand all elderly staff as lacking either the capability or willingness to change or to make valuable contributions to their organisation. In fact, some leaders regarded experienced older personnel as valuable members of staff insofar as they are able to distil the significant aspects of current practice that need to be changed. A principal argued that:

> Working with experienced staff, you get the experience of years. You get a lot of [experienced] staff who are willing to look at change, or look at a program and say, 'Ok, let's look at this and let's change it this way. We can do a short cut or we can do something that will make it easier for us.'

Some educational leaders noted that while replacing older personnel is complex, absence of 'new blood' may lead to a lack of creative energy and enthusiasm in the school. A principal put the problem clearly and succinctly:

> I think one of the other things that I find that I'm challenged by, and I'm sure everybody else is too, is the whole issue about the ageing work force. We've got an ageing work force and because we've got changing budgets, we've got shrinking recruitment, which doesn't bring in the new staff; we've got, therefore, less injection of enthusiasm, and youth.

A principal warned, however, that staff have to be prepared to move on from the status quo and embrace change, if they are to survive in contemporary schools:

> I am talking about change in every facet, externally driven change, yes. Change in people's own lives and belief systems . . . I mean there are changes in people's lives, and this impinges upon their work. So change, in its broader sense, but certainly there are external forces in terms of curriculum, in terms of school . . . issues where there is a lot of change happening. They are pretty significant [in terms of] their impact.

This tension between opting for the status quo instead of change and development generates numerous ethical tensions for leaders.

While they must respect the traditions and practices of long-serving staff, they are also ethically responsible for keeping their school and its teaching approaches 'up-to-date' and constantly improving.

Dealing with tensions: Lessons from leaders

The educational leaders in this study were asked to reflect on the tension situations and dilemmas in which they had been involved, and which many of them described so vividly, and to identify lessons they had learned from them. The following are paraphrased from some of the most pertinent and insightful responses:

- There is no 'one best way' for determining which side(s) of a tension situation you should choose. You have to examine the facts of the situation carefully, and then use your rational thought, wisdom and judgement to strike a balance among sometimes conflicting values and interests.
- There are no simple and easy answers when dealing with people and value conflict. The pursuit of a rational approach to decision-making is recommended.
- You have to be true to yourself and live your values. You have to live with yourself at the end of the day. Honesty and openness, when deciding on such tensions, is always the best policy. Deceptiveness and playing politics are condemned.
- It is better to deal with a difficult situation sooner rather than later; putting off difficult steps in a process of decision-making does not make the difficulties disappear.
- Sometimes, there needs to be a clinical approach to situations; compassionate leadership should be the norm but, often, a less soft approach must be considered, in the interest of the common good.
- Always be guided, when making ethical decisions, by what you believe is 'right and good'.
- When the going gets tough and you know you're right, you need to stick with your decision. It takes moral courage to stand up for what you believe to be right.
- Decisions will be different depending on the persons involved and the mitigating circumstances.

- Welfare of the organisation may necessitate tough top-down decision-making. While good does not always come from getting consensus first, those who have to implement decisions must have input into making them.
- The easy option in difficult situations is to do nothing. Leaders, however, must speak up against injustice. They are duty bound to follow ethical and moral courses of action.
- It seems easier to arrange for the transfer of ineffective staff or ignore them altogether, than to try to dismiss them. However, leaders should 'bite the bullet' and tackle the problem of inefficient staff members sooner rather than later.
- Leaders need to 'walk the talk' and do what they say they are going to do. It is not good enough to say all the right things but, in times of stress, practise entirely different principles.
- It is important to trust the basic 'goodness' of people. Leaders have to give trust to get it in return.
- At the end of the day, you need to own the decision and be able to give sound reasons for it.

It is usually better to approach a tension situation with a *both/and* rather than an *either/or* mindset. Often it is not a matter of the individual *versus* the group or common good; or loyalty *versus* honesty, but that consideration be given in decision-making to the individual *and* the common good as well as to honesty *and* loyalty.

Leaders need to be able to map complex situations that involve tensions, and apply frameworks that help them make sense of this complexity. The elements of such a framework are identified and discussed in the next chapter.

Key ideas for reflection

The real challenges for educational leaders are usually characterised by tensions between and among people – especially with regard to their philosophies, values, interests and preferences.

Tensions usually reflect the quality of the relationships between and among people. Rarely, however, can issues involving complex human relationships be resolved by neat, logical and linear management processes or tools, no matter how systematically or how thoroughly they are applied.

A close scrutiny of many of the cases presented in this chapter demonstrates that expectations, perspectives and opinions may differ when the human elements of a tension situation are considered. Usually, *either/or* thinking that adopts a one-dimensional response will not encompass the complexity of real human dramas. *Both/and* responses that take into consideration contradictions and opposites are more likely to lead to satisfactory outcomes.

Questions for reflection

Briefly describe a recent critical incident involving tensions where you had to make difficult ethical choices:

- What happened in the situation (the facts of the matter)?
- Who were involved and what were their possible intentions/motivations?
- What were the key dynamics and processes in the incident/event?
- What tensions were experienced, and by whom?
- What choices did you and others make, and with what consequences?
- What lessons did you learn from the incident/event?

Reflect on and analyse the incident from a both/and perspective

When identifying the tensions involved, refer especially to those related to: common good *and* individual rights; care *and* rules; long-term *and* short-term; loyalty *and* honesty; service *and* economic rationalism; status quo *and* change and development. Not all these tensions will apply to every critical incident so choose those that are relevant and useful in understanding and resolving the critical incident.

Alternatively, you may wish to use one of the cases reported in this chapter that is similar to a situation you had to deal with. Feel free to embellish the case by including elements of the situation you had to resolve.

Remember: the more complex and multidimensional the case the more challenging it will be to apply *both/and* approaches to resolving it.

Chapter 4

A framework for analysing tensions

The challenges and tensions faced by educational leaders in this study, and discussed in chapters 2 and 3, were complex and multidimensional. It was evident that most of the respondents in the study had no rigorous and systematic method for analysing and responding to these tensions. It seems clear that educational leaders require frames of reference for making choices that can encompass seemingly opposite considerations, values and ethical positions. This need is not well accepted, never mind understood or appreciated, by a majority of those who study and practice educational leadership and management. The traditional perspective of a world of certainty and precision that can be controlled through management techniques and strategies still tends to dominate educational leadership thinking and practice.

Frameworks are needed that help educational leaders appreciate that 'the opposites are necessary to each other' (Handy, 1994, p. 48). Handy advocates that leaders must learn to frame the confusion and find pathways through the paradoxes by understanding what is actually happening in a particular situation and by learning to be different (p. 3). They must break the bonds imposed by dualistic *either/or* mindsets and try to cultivate *both/and* thinking and decision-making approaches.

Proposed framework for analysing tensions

In a significant research study entitled 'The Double-Headed Arrow: Australian Managers in the Business Context of Asia', English (1995) referred to paradox as a tension situation that is primarily characterised by relationship and complementarity rather than polar opposites. He defined tension as '*two contrasting phenomena in a relationship that embodies both competition and complementarity*' (p. 58, italics in original). A challenge for educational leaders is that tensions often represent 'phenomena separated at an arbitrary point on a continuum. **Sensitivity ↔ insensitivity** is such a tension – there is no unequivocal division between sensitivity and insensitivity' (pp. 58–59). The resolution of tensions, English concluded, is a matter of good judgement that is '. . . heavily influenced by the nature of the judge' (p. 60). He continues by arguing that, in the context of managerial work, the analysis and interpretation of tensions ' . . . is grounded in experience and the perceptual frameworks that actors take to that experience'.

He recommended that leaders should analyse tension situations, not in terms of contradiction, polarity, and *either/or* frames but in terms of a *relationship* that encompasses both competition and complementarity. They should, he says, determine as best they can, the qualities and conditions of relationships in each situation. In this way they can better understand and manage a change situation (usually characterised by uncertainty and confusion) by building a profile of the tensions – in Handy's terms they are framing the confusion – as presented in Figure 4.2.

A tension situation can best be characterised by a *double-headed arrow* (English, 1995, p. 276) as shown in Figure 4.1. Often polar opposites are actually in a complex relationship, and influences are rarely one-way. Instead of being mutually exclusive, most seeming opposites are 'in tension', characterised partly by competition and partly by complementarity: 'You can't have one without the other'. 'Tension', as used here, does not have to be the type of tension that emanates from interpersonal conflict, even though such tensions may also be present.

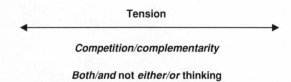

Figure 4.1 Double-headed arrow (Adapted from English, 1995)

By emphasising the relationship and complementarity, instead of the seeming contradictions and opposites, leaders and managers have a better chance of influencing the direction and intensity of the positive elements of the tension (English, 1995). Otherwise, they may opt for the *either/or* approach, perhaps believing that the opposing forces are mutually exclusive and incompatible, thereby creating a win-lose situation.

Let us take an example in which a teacher has contributed quality service for over 25 years but is currently performing at a much lower level. A number of tensions, identified earlier in the cases related to teacher performance, are inherent in such a situation. Decision-makers require frameworks for dealing with these tensions. We can analyse the tensions in this situation, using the concept of the double-headed arrow, in a way that will help leaders frame and analyse the tensions. All six of the major tensions discussed in chapter 3 may be seen in this single situation:

1 considerations for the **individual** (the teacher) *and* the **common good** (the clients/students);
2 **care** (showing compassion and a caring attitude to the teacher) *and* **rules** (following the 'letter of the law' with regard to the rules on performance appraisal);
3 **long-term** (interests of teacher and students) *and* **short-term** (the quick but not necessarily easy way would be to dismiss the staff member);
4 **loyalty** (to the teacher for long service) *and* **honesty** (about current performance in the interests of justice);
5 **service** (providing the best possible support for the teacher and teaching for the students) *and* **economic rationalism** (making most thrifty use of resources, including other staff's time); and
6 **status quo** (it is often easier to leave things as they are but this will not usually solve the problem) *and* **change and development** (an obvious option is to provide the staff member with professional development opportunities).

If we approach this situation with an *either/or* mindset, then we may tend to see the issues in terms of only one of the polarities, for instance, in terms of the common good without due consideration for the individual rights of the staff member. Or we may decide that

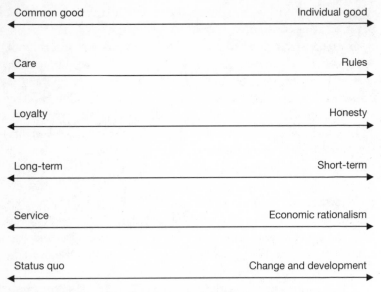

Figure 4.2 Framing the tensions: Look for the complementary

'rules are rules' and therefore compassion isn't really an option. However, if we adopt a *both/and* mindset we will look for the complementarity in these tensions and try to choose options that reflect a balanced consideration for both rules and caring. We can depict our options related to these tensions in diagram form (see Figure 4.2). In this way we can better frame a difficult, multidimensional situation and make a more enlightened decision. In the end, however, judgements have to be made to resolve the tensions.

By applying each of the double-headed arrows to the situation encountered, a profile of the tension situation emerges which is more likely to result in informed choices that are responsive to the complexity of the problem. Judgements will still have to be made using the best available information and a framework for decision-making that is ethical and value-based (see chapter 6).

Without an approach such as this it is easy to feel overwhelmed and frustrated with the complexity of the situation, and to respond in simplistic and inadequately informed ways. The framework helps simplify the complex, by illuminating the key dimensions of a particular situation. It helps the decision-maker identify the multiple perspectives, value positions and differences in experiences so typical of individuals and groups involved in contentious situations in organisational settings. While the application of this framework will not deliver a 'cut-and-dried' answer, it will assist educational leaders to make good decisions in difficult situations, by encouraging them to consider relationships and complementarity, rather than conflict and disagreement, thereby enabling them to balance the tensions for a positive outcome. Equally importantly, the framework will support leaders to communicate the reasons for their decisions well, so that even if stakeholders are unhappy with the outcome, they know all aspects were taken into consideration.

It is important to note that not all the dimensions identified in Figure 4.2 will apply to every tension situation. Educational leaders will need to determine which ones are relevant and useful in analysing such situations. In the case of the student who received a blue slip as a penalty for misbehaviour within one week of a major regional athletics carnival (in chapter 3), only three of the dimensions were addressed directly by the principal and these are depicted in Figure 4.3.

Figure 4.3 Framing the tensions: A specific case

The decision was made to allow the student to compete even though it was against the rules, thereby emphasising the care side of the care–rules continuum. The decision also gave greater weight to the individual good of the student over the common good of the other students because by breaking the rules a precedent was established which could have been criticised because other students who had committed similar offences in the past were excluded from athletic competition. As well, the decision considered the long-term consequences to the student whose self-concept was so dependent on athletic performance over the short-term implications of excluding him from the competition, even though it was setting a precedent.

Often in cases like this, decision-makers have no frameworks to help them identify the multidimensionality of a challenging situation, or the type of tensions involved. The application of a framework like the ones in Figures 4.2 and 4.3 helps make sense of complex situations and highlights *both/and* approaches to decision-making. In the end, judgement is still called for in reaching a resolution to the tensions involved, but the framework helps clarify what exactly is under consideration.

The framework in action

In many of the complex cases already cited in this book, it might be tempting for decision-makers to quickly jump to conclusions, to blame one side or another, to opt for one set of values over another simply because they more closely reflect or support their own assumptions and values. It is often easier to adopt an *either/or* approach because this can reduce the confusion and frustration of dealing with competing value positions or unpopular alternatives. This framework, based on the concept of the double-headed arrow, reminds the decision-maker that '... *the inclusion of competing value perspectives may be essential to adaptive success*' (Heifetz, 1994, p. 23, italics in original). Finding the simple solution, or the one right answer, is often neither tenable nor effective.

In the incident about possible student involvement in drugs described and discussed in chapter 3, there were some, including teachers and parents, who did not know all of the facts of the situation and there were also sharp differences of opinion between and among groups (teachers and parents) as to how the girls should be dealt with, especially considering that some of the girls were nearing the completion of their academic careers. The principal who reported the case indicated that there were a number of difficult and complex issues to be considered, including competing values. He identified these as:

Valuing the need to create a safe environment for the remainder of the student body; wanting to also deal with these girls justly and to enable them to move on from their mistake; protecting the interests of the parents; and also creating an environment in which staff felt that there was still a level of discipline within the student body and that we weren't going to give the wrong messages about that.

The framework of the double-headed arrow can be usefully applied to this case. It is important for the principal to start by trying to establish the key significant facts in the situation. Often this is best achieved through open dialogue, though privacy issues must be dealt with as necessary. The idea is to start with the facts that are not in dispute (finding a touchstone) and then build from there. There may also be values, ideas and opinions that are not in dispute, and these are also important touchstones. Finding the touchstone(s) is the key. As most people who have had to deal with such situations know, it may be impossible to determine the full truth of the situation. This usually means that informed (but not necessarily fully informed) judgement will be called for at some stage.

There are obviously many dimensions that would benefit from analysis using the double-headed arrow. There are individual and common good considerations in the situation. What is in the best interests of individual students? What about the effects on the school population if the sanctions for these girls are regarded as inadequate or unfair? A decision that is in the short-term interests of the school or of particular classes in which the girls are taught may not be in the long-term interests of the girls and their parents. And perhaps more importantly, rules are rules and drugs are strictly prohibited. It is usually well known to students that being in possession of drugs in school, or being involved with them outside school, attracts severe sanctions.

How then can the decision-maker (or decision-makers) in this case apply a degree of care and compassion to the resolution of this situation when the rules are so clear? Not all of the dimensions of a tension situation will always involve contestable values dualities. In this case the girls were dealt with on a case-by-case basis. This then raises a concern over the principle of justice (discussed in the next chapter) if some are treated more leniently than others. However, the details of each girl's involvement differed, so the manner of dealing with them also differed. This is why the proposed method for ethical decision-making in chapter 6 emphasises collecting and understanding, as far as is possible, the facts of the situation. A decision based on false or unsubstantiated information is not going to be a wise one.

The framework can help the decision-maker focus on and analyse the numerous dimensions inherent in the situation. The concepts of relationship and complementarity help to remind the decision-maker that in a situation where facts, values, ideas and opinions are all in tension, it is essential to look for and build on the common ground or touchstone.

This discussion on the use of the framework in the example above has focused, primarily, on a single decision-maker, for example an educational leader such as a school principal, applying it to a difficult situation involving tensions. However, groups can also use this framework successfully. In the case discussed above it is clear that different teachers have different points of view on the facts and on the possible alternative solutions. Parents, too, have divergent views on the seriousness of the situation and on possible alternative solutions.

Using the framework to build group understanding

The concepts of relationship and complementarity should be emphasised in any group analysis of the situation. I have used the double-headed arrows with groups to build a profile of the numerous dimensions inherent in a particular challenging situation and, mostly, these groups have been surprised to see the complexity and multidimensionality of the situation spread out before them. I have emphasised in such discussions that what often appears to be polar opposites, or equally unwelcome possibilities as with a dilemma (for example, with regard to values, perspectives or opinions) usually lend themselves to a more positive analysis using the concept of the touchstone, and to a greater appreciation of the usefulness of *both/and* thinking as opposed to *either/or* thinking.

The use of the framework not only helps frame the confusion, as Handy (1994) recommended, it can also help a group approach tension situations with a positive mindset, helping them concentrate on common ground instead of differences. As with any group analysis approach, it would need to be used with parent groups with care and good judgement. Issues related to drugs, as well as other serious student discipline issues as discussed in chapter 3, can generate much heated debate and an unwillingness to compromise. I would recommend that, when using this framework with such groups, the idea of a group search for the touchstone(s), relationship(s) and complementarity in tension situations should be the primary agenda item, and that this should be reinforced by pointing out the usefulness of *both/and* thinking. While there are no guarantees of general agreement, never mind consensus, on such occasions, it seems sensible to identify common ground, no matter how small, and build from there.

A constraint in all group decision situations, especially when dealing with sensitive information or when issues of privacy are a concern, is that it may not be advisable or wise to share the known facts of the situation. Obviously, then, it will be difficult, if not impossible, for the group to come up with a well-informed decision.

Another consideration is that identification and analysis of tensions, and their subsequent resolution, involve the use of good judgement, and that can be greatly influenced by the background experiences of the judge. Educational leaders can temper their possible biases and prejudices by entering into open discussion and dialogue with key stakeholders, by developing sympathetic listening skills, and by learning to suspend their own judgements until all, or most, of the significant facts of the situation are known and key perspectives and opinions are canvassed. The wisdom of groups should never be underestimated.

Even in situations that appear to be intractable, where opinions seem to be diametrically opposed, there is usually some degree of touchstone or common ground. Considering the tensions methodically in this way will assist educational leaders to discover these touchstones. Once they have identified them, they can build on them, accepting of course that there will continue to be differences of perspective and opinion. Usually, there is no one solution in such challenging situations; resolution based on good judgement is the most likely outcome.

With practice, this approach can become a habit of mind applied with the speed of thought. Although some people may always prefer to sketch a rough diagram as an *aide-mémoire*, once you get into the *both/and* mode of thinking you will not generally need to apply elaborate diagrams or engage in step-by-step processes. As always, it is important for educational leaders to take the concept of the framework and apply it in a way that works for them. A slightly more formal approach may be necessary with groups.

An important added consideration when analysing the type of challenges discussed in chapters 2 and 3 is that such complex situations involving people in disagreement or tension usually have ethical and value-based dimensions, and these have to be factored in when making decisions to resolve the situations. An ethics and values approach to decision-making in such situations is discussed in the next chapter.

Key ideas for reflection

A tension situation can best be characterised by a *double-headed arrow* showing the relationship between seeming opposites. Many of the tensions identified in chapter 3 represent values, perspectives and opinions separated at an arbitrary point on a continuum; for example, individual good ↔ common good is such a tension. Part of the difficulty in making a decision involving this continuum is that there is no unequivocal, indisputable division between individual interests and the common good. The decision-maker has to make a judgement as to which point on the continuum will deliver the best solution to the tension.

Questions for reflection

Take the analysis of the critical incident you described at the end of chapter 3 to a new level by focusing on the relationships and complementarities in the tensions (as depicted in Figures 4.1, 4.2 and 4.3). This will help you better understand and apply the concept of the double-headed arrow, as well as *both/and* approaches to resolving tensions in real-life situations.

- What are the key tensions in the situation?
- Where are the touchstones, in terms of the facts, in each of the tensions?
- How can you build on these touchstones to influence the intensity and direction of the positive elements of the tension situation?
- What are several different ways that you might be able to resolve this situation?
- What is the best possible resolution of this situation at this time?

Chapter 5

Values and ethics in decision-making

The tensions identified in earlier chapters are part of the fabric of life and work in service organisations, such as schools. They can be very challenging, even frustrating, but cannot be wished away or ignored. Part of the responsibility of working in a service environment is to engage in positive, productive and ethical ways with these tensions. Decisions have to be made based on informed judgement, and educational leaders need to develop processes that will provide them with 'a foundation for probing the ethical depths of each situation that calls for a judgement' (Rebore, 2001, p. 31). The framework described and discussed in chapter 4 will help educational leaders to analyse challenging situations and better understand their complexity and multidimensionality. The framework assists educational leaders to consider multiple contestable values dualities, as represented by the double-headed arrow (e.g. care ↔ rules), to understand tension situations. In addition, however, educational leaders will benefit from understanding how values and ethics can help inform such decisions. That understanding is the focus of this chapter.

Values and decision-making

Values are important for determining our sense of who we are. They develop over time and are influenced by family, education, peers and a whole range of experiences, both good and bad, that have helped shape us. Even though we share many of our values with others, there will always be differences; whether in the degree of intensity with which we hold our values or the way we prioritise them. These differences can lead to dispute, disagreement, and even outright conflict.

I may believe that truth is the most important value to be preserved in a certain situation, such as the one described earlier for the students who were asked by the teacher to enter other students' marks into the computer. On the other hand, *you* may believe that loyalty to the teacher ought to predominate. Both of us presumably believe that truth and loyalty are important values, but we differ on how they ought to be prioritised in this case. We might call this type of problem a tension characterised by a 'difference of opinion'. Sometimes the difference may not be over which value is more important, but whether or not an agreed value is best served by a particular line of action. *You* may believe that justice is best served by doing things this way, while *I* believe it will be better served that way. This sort of problem is described as a choice between right and right (Kidder, 1995). Such choices and differences of opinion occur on a regular basis, giving considerations of values and ethics the reputation of being contentious.

This conundrum of right-versus-right is a quandary often faced by leaders who have to make choices in situations where values and ethical considerations are paramount (Kidder, 1995). Kidder stated: 'Tough choices, typically, are those that pit one right value against another' (p. 16). He pointed out that right-versus-right values are at the heart of most difficult choices in life and work situations. While there are numerous right-versus-wrong situations, they are, for the most part, more easily discernible, and therefore more easily dealt with by honest, well-intentioned people than are right-versus-right situations. The most difficult choices faced by leaders are so difficult 'precisely because each side is firmly rooted in . . . core values' (Kidder, 1995, p. 18).

Such choices usually present tensions between competing values (the double-headed arrow) where each can be interpreted as 'right' and justified in a given situation. Many of the tensions faced by leaders in this study fall into this category of right-and-right choices, such as:

1 the rights of the individual *versus* those of the group or community;

2 the exercise of compassion *versus* rigidly following the rules;
3 the provision of a quality service *versus* the efficient use of scarce resources; and
4 doing one's duty *versus* doing the just thing.

Often there are deep ethical issues embedded in these tensions, which need to be considered when making decisions about how to resolve them.

Ethics and decision-making

Educational leaders must incorporate ethical analysis as part of their thinking and reasoning because ethics is 'at the core of a given human enterprise . . . [it] addresses issues through a disciplined way of thinking' and it helps answer the 'question of why' in relation to complex and contested human dilemmas (Rebore, 2001, pp. 7–8).

The challenge in ethical analysis is that it involves values, choices, dilemmas, grey areas and character. We are constantly challenged in life to make choices about the kinds of people we are going to be and the kinds of actions we will or will not take. Ethical decision-making requires a keen sensitivity to the implications and consequences of particular choices when the facts of the matter may be unclear, or even contradictory. It also requires a knowledge of how to apply different ethical viewpoints in everyday decision-making.

The complexity of ethical issues is evident time and again in the responses of leaders in this study. Ethical considerations and challenges are especially evident in areas where leaders must take responsibility for their actions even though it is not clear to them how best to act in a particular situation. Examples of major challenges faced by leaders in the study include: the need to initiate action or to follow through with disciplinary actions, despite personal cost to themselves; and how to prioritise organisational needs and values in organisational restructuring over the needs and values of individuals, even their own.

An example of the first type of challenge is the case of the principal who had to deal with an elderly member of staff who was showing increasing signs of dementia. The principal had known the staff member and her husband for many years and his initial approach to her husband backfired when positions became entrenched. The principal had to overcome his own positive personal regard for the staff member and her husband in the interests of the students under her care. He indicated that 'in the final analysis, the needs and rights of the students were the deciding factor in removing her from most of her teaching'. While care for the students was uppermost in his mind, he also felt a duty of care to a staff member who had served the students and the school very well for a number of years. There was a personal cost involved in the decision he made.

The case of the educational leader who had to hand out white envelopes inviting staff to accept a redundancy package is an example of this second type of challenge. This leader clearly indicated that he had great difficulty doing this; 'I'm the messenger. I've got to stand up in front of the staff and say that this is what we are doing and this is why we are doing it and, at the same time, not believing that it was the best thing in every aspect.'

The first example seems to be a matter of making a difficult choice to do what is right (e.g. apply the rules fairly to all who are subject to disciplinary action), even though it may be at a cost to the individual being disciplined. This usually concerns a tension between the good of the individual versus the common good. The second example can also be viewed as a choice between two rights. Organisations, or at least those who have the responsibility of leading them, have the right to respond to their organisation's needs, goals and strategic purposes, even though these, at times, may conflict with the needs, goals, desires and strategic intentions of individuals within the organisation. Leaders are challenged to find a balance between these two 'rights'. As will be discussed later in this chapter and in chapter 6, leaders need ethical and value-based frameworks for making good decisions in such situations.

The numerous examples in recent times of organisations' leaders who seem to have forgotten or ignored values and ethics in the choices they made (e.g. Enron, WorldCom, HIH) seem to reflect Kidder's (1995) category of *moral temptation* (right-versus-wrong) rather than right-versus-right.

We are constantly faced with making choices. Some of these are trivial, such as what outfit to wear or what meal to select in a restaurant. Others are important, such as what shares to buy as a long-term investment or what house to invest in. Still others are fundamental, such as what kind of person I want to be.

These latter choices are 'ultimate choices', since they really shape us and our destiny (Singer, 1979). Singer gives the example of Ivan Boesky and his decision to get involved in insider trading (p. 4), which clearly appears to involve a choice between right and wrong. Many of the choices made by leaders who later ended up in court (e.g. from Enron, WorldCom, HIH) would seem to involve issues of moral temptation as well as legal sanction and, given many of the court findings, seem clearly classifiable as 'wrong'.

However, sometimes we are faced with the dilemma of making a choice between two 'wrongs' – whatever we do seems to bring unwelcome consequences – hence the expression 'damned if you do, damned if you don't'. In the novel and movie *Sophie's Choice*, the situation in which Sophie had to choose which of her two children should be sent to death in the gas ovens epitomises such a dilemma.

Sometimes the choices we must make to live up to our value system will not be confusing or impossible, like Sophie's. They will be stark and clear, but will require real courage if we are to go through with them. These are the ones that demand character on our part. The ethical thing to do may test our courage. Examples include the problems associated with 'whistle blowing' or the refusal to follow unethical instructions from a manager or a valued client. The issue of moral courage can be seen clearly in some of the interview responses of the leaders in the study, quoted earlier, especially those where principals had to 'bite the bullet' and take action against those with long loyal service, who were sometimes their personal friends.

As stated earlier, ethical choices often reflect grey areas where there are no simple *either/or* resolutions. Grey areas are those in which laws, policies or guidelines are not clear. As a result, individuals may be unsure how to proceed. If possible, in such grey situations one ought to clarify the facts of the matter, but if the situation still remains unclear, or if an urgent decision has to be made, then all one can do is one's best. Judgement is called for, at the end of the day.

As long as we do our best, mostly all we can be charged with is making a mistake or an error of judgement. Having a clear sense of what one is facing – value choice, difference in perspectives, dilemma, or grey area – makes the ethical issue a little easier to understand as well as easier to discuss and, ultimately, manage.

Discussing ethical issues with other key stakeholders is usually a wise strategy. However, it must be recognised that ethical dialogue usually reflects a variety of voices, all of whom have a right to be heard and believe they are right. Once we start talking about values, we have to confront the fact that, in a society like ours, there is no essential agreement on these values. We live in a multicultural and pluralistic society in which there is no one set of agreed prevailing values and there is often a general reluctance to talk about one's own values.

One of the functions of ethics in society, however, is to enable us to enter into dialogue with others about the appropriateness of human decisions and actions. Ethics is not about my belief that X is good and Y is bad. Ethics begins when we start giving reasons for our views about X and Y. To explore these beliefs and reasons further, we will now explore different approaches to ethics and their possible relevance and application to decision situations.

Approaches to ethics

This chapter attempts to introduce and discuss the essence of major ethical theories and principles for busy practitioners who need a quick reference guide for ethical decision-making in tension-filled situations. I recommend, however, that all educational leaders study ethics in some depth, and their implications for, and applications to, decision-making processes and making judgements, especially when the choices are not clear cut. Numerous books on ethics and ethical leadership provide detailed discussions and analyses of ethical principles and theories, for example, Rebore (2001) *The ethics of educational leadership*, Beckner (2004) *Ethics for educational leaders* or Shapiro and Stefkovich (2005) *Ethical leadership and decision making in education*.

Some people approach ethics by means of a theory, which they see as giving them an understanding of ethics and ethical issues. They seek one theory which could encompass all dimensions of ethics and enable people to find a sound answer to any ethical issue.

The two major theoretical approaches in ethics are deontology and utilitarianism.

Deontology (rule-based thinking or 'doing one's duty')

This ethical theory derives its name from the Greek word *deon*, meaning 'duty'. The origin of this approach to ethics is found in the writings of the German philosopher Immanuel Kant (1724–1804). Kant insisted that we can know our moral duty by *rational reflection*, and if we are to be ethical then we must fulfil the demands of duty. Rational reflection, then, becomes the focus of the individual's autonomous choice to live in accordance with the demands of moral duty. In fact, doing one's duty becomes the motivation for action.

A renowned deontologist of the 1930s, W. D. Ross, in his book *The right and the good*, considered the question: 'Which actions are morally superior, those done for duty or those done for love?' His conclusion was that 'the desire to do one's duty is the morally best motive'. This kind of view can lead us to the conclusion that parents caring for their children act in a morally superior way when they do so because it is their duty rather than because they love them.

This ethical theory has the advantage of offering clear and absolute positions on a range of issues such as euthanasia, truthfulness, honouring of promises and so on. This is what Kidder (1995) describes as 'rule-based thinking'.

Utilitarianism (ends-based thinking or 'consequentialism')

The other great ethical theory derives from the writings of the English philosophers, Jeremy Bentham (1748–1832) and John Stuart Mill (1806–1873). The basic insight of utilitarianism is that the morality of an action is to be evaluated in the light of its consequences. Hence the other name associated with this approach is consequentialism.

Probably the expression that best sums up this ethical theory is one that is quite familiar in the field of economics. It is the demand that one should strive to bring about 'the greatest good for the greatest number'. The ethics of an action then are determined by an estimation of whether or not it has increased or decreased the sum of happiness for the greatest number of people. The focus is on the consequences rather than the action itself. Kidder (1995) describes this as 'ends-based thinking'.

A major criticism of this approach is that it fails to pay sufficient account to the needs of individuals. Nor is it particularly concerned with the question of rights. Another problem is whether to focus on immediate or long-term results. It also has the complication that we cannot always foresee the results of all our actions. How can we really know the potential consequences of our proposed actions or choices?

In more recent discussions of ethics, there is a move to focus on care rather than to simply look at actions and consequences.

Care-based thinking

Some of this change of focus from consequences to care has come from feminist criticism of Kantian and Kohlbergian approaches. It has been particularly developed within the nursing ethics literature, as it seems to harmonise with the fundamental driving force of this profession in terms of *care for patients*. It is, however, equally applicable to other professions of a pastoral orientation. Teachers, in particular, are aware of their duty of care for students.

There is no doubt that care must be an important guiding principle in ethical decision-making. But is it the best principle to resolve difficult issues and complex problems clearly? From the responses of leaders in this study, it would seem that it is not always clear how care is best exercised in a complex issue. Trying to decide how to do the right thing and, at the same time, exercise compassion for individuals can be very challenging. There are times, for example in cases of child abuse or sexual harassment, when rules, regulations and legal imperatives may have to be weighted heavily in the decision-making process. The answer, of course, may not be found by a simple appeal to one overriding principle.

Principlism

Many practitioners are often not satisfied with the solutions to ethical problems offered by deontology or utilitarianism. They feel that these theories are too abstracted from the complexities of real-life situations. The sole consideration of actions or consequences does not seem to take sufficient notice of all the factors that might influence a final choice or decision. They have then suggested that we need to come down to some set of second level principles ('principlism') to guide us in greater detail (Josephson, 2002).

There is no one agreed set of principles but among the commonly suggested ones are the following:

- autonomy;
- common good; and
- justice.

Autonomy

This broad principle means that in making ethical decisions, especially involving adults, we should respect them as individuals with autonomous rights to make their own decisions and shape their own lives. While children in their early years need to be guided, and often have their decisions made for them by parents, as they come to adulthood parental control should relax leaving them to be responsible for their own lives. In school life, especially in upper primary and secondary schools, we are often dealing with autonomous young adults and ought to show them the respect that is their due. This principle finds expression in many ways when dealing with people: not interfering with their freedom; telling them the truth; supplying them with all the information they need to be able to make their own decisions; treating them as equal human beings; and respecting their rights.

Common good

If we are to be ethical, then as far as possible our aim should be to do good to a maximum number of people and to refrain from doing harm. However, it is not always clear in practice what 'doing good for the greatest number' might involve. It could be that the ideal of the common good is difficult to realise in a multicultural society. Also, as was discussed in chapter 3, the interests of the common good (e.g. class of students) may conflict with the interests of individuals (various individual students) and a caring profession, such as teaching, needs to balance all these interests.

The reverse principle of not harming is perhaps clearer. It means that we should refrain from actions that will result in harm to people. Generally speaking, it means that we are not justified in taking actions that directly harm others.

Justice

This is a major principle in ethics, and requires some more detailed treatment than the previous principles. There is a vast amount of literature on justice, particularly on distributive justice, meaning the distribution of burdens and benefits within society.

The philosophical concerns about justice have been how to define it accurately and how to devise a system of justice that can operate satisfactorily in society. The basic notion of justice is that each person should be given his or her due, in a way that does not harm society in general. In approaching justice, some will want to emphasise the primacy of the individual and his/her rights, while others will emphasise the good of the community.

Despite the fact that we may believe that all people are created equal, when we observe society we soon realise that people are, in fact, not equal. There are vast differences in talent, abilities and social situations, This disparity can be explained in terms of the genetic and social lottery. For some, their advantage stems from genetic factors such as basic good health and intelligence. Others owe their advantage to the social situation into which they were born, such as wealthy, well-adjusted parents who were able to provide them with a sound education and a good financial start in life. Those less well off may regard themselves as unfortunate, but no injustice, necessarily, has been done to them. Some will say that is simply the way things are – unfortunate but not unfair.

This is part of the lottery of life. In the strict sense, they say, there is nothing unfair about their situation. Others will say that while this may be true, justice demands that something be done to offset their disadvantage.

While principlism has much to offer, another – much older – approach to ethics is also very relevant to ethical decision-making in educational organisations.

Rational wisdom (based on Aristotle's thinking)

Many think that the approaches just discussed do not provide an adequate response to the complexity inherent in many ethical tensions. The *theories*, they argue, are too remote from real-life complexity and the *principles* often are in conflict with one another; for instance, doing good to someone in a particular situation may conflict with the demands of justice for someone else. These ways of applying ethics often leave unanswered questions, and this has led to a continued search for a more complete approach to ethics. In this search, many are returning to the ideas of some of the ancient philosophers, particularly those of Aristotle.

Aristotle's first principle of ethics is not an action-guide, but simply the goal we all seek – to live well, to live a good life, to achieve fulfilment, to flourish, to be happy while we live. The emphasis in his approach is on the good of the person performing the action. Behaviour that makes our lives good is considered virtuous, and behaviour making our lives bad is considered worthless. The assumption is that most people want to live well, so this desire for a good life becomes the starting point of ethics.

There will always be disagreements about the particularities of what constitutes a good life, but there is a large area of agreement shared among people. The best indicator of this agreement lies in what we teach our children. We want our children to be happy and try to teach them how to achieve happiness (Deveterre, 1995, p. 20). We teach them to be truthful, caring, fair and tolerant because we want them to have a good (virtuous) life.

However, in order to work out what is really good for us as individuals and as members of society, we need to develop our skills of ethical judgement. This requires the virtue of *wisdom*, which Aristotle describes in terms of knowing how to respond appropriately in different sets of circumstances. The work of ethics is to help us clarify what truly constitutes a good life and then deliberate on how to achieve this in whatever set of circumstances confront us. So, for Aristotle, it is not just a matter of having the right overarching theory or having a set of principles or rules to apply, it is a question of choosing to strive for the correct end *and* to find the right means to achieve that end. This requires the development of virtues, or habits, which enable us to act in a consistent fashion. There are two kinds of virtues: moral and intellectual.

The moral virtues include justice, courage and temperance, which Aristotle regarded as 'golden means' between two opposing vices of excess and deficiency. For example, he regarded courage as the golden mean between the excess of 'rashness' and the deficiency of 'cowardice'. He recommended moderation in all things, with the ultimate aim of being a virtuous person, that is, a person of good character, in order to lead a virtuous life – one that is good, happy and fulfilling.

The intellectual virtues, which Aristotle regarded as of a higher order than the moral virtues, are wisdom and prudence. These are now discussed at some length, as they are more directly related to an understanding of rational wisdom.

Wisdom, according to Aristotle, is the kind of knowledge needed for science and an understanding of things. It helps us understand our world. It is the kind of knowledge that is typical of an observer trying to understand an issue.

This form of wisdom is referred to by Groome (1998, p. 288) as a 'reasonable wisdom', which engages the whole person, and 'encourages integrity between knower and knowledge'. Wisdom includes, but goes beyond, knowledge and reason, and it constitutes *'the realization of knowledge in life-giving ways – for self, others, and the world'* (italics in original). A reasonable wisdom constitutes a 'wisdom way of knowing', which, in essence, is 'knowing with an ethic' (Groome, 1998, p. 288). It also constitutes a quest for truth, which has *'cognitive, relational*, and *moral* aspects' (Groome, 1998, p. 301, italics in original).

The cognitive aspect of truth points to what 'rings true to experience', 'makes sense' to one's way of thinking, and 'works' for life' (Groome, 1998, p. 303). The relational aspect of truth refers to loyalty and faithfulness in commitments and relationships. The moral aspect of truth constitutes a commitment to 'living the truth', as truth must be '. . . one's way of life' (Groome, 1998, p. 304).

Prudence, on the other hand, is a practical type of reasoning: the kind of knowledge we need for doing things. In Aristotle's way of thinking, it is the kind of knowledge necessary to direct a military operation, or practise medicine, or play a musical instrument, or to live our lives. It is the practical knowledge we need to figure out how to live our lives and to achieve personal happiness.

Prudence is not just shrewdness or keeping an eye on the main chance. It is the deliberation and thinking necessary for one to work out what is the appropriate thing to do in any given set of circumstances. As the circumstances change, so will one's judgement of what is or is not appropriate action. This does not mean that one is cut free of any principles or ethical rules. They still have bearing on the ethics of one's action, but prudence involves knowing which rules or principles to apply in any given set of circumstances, or how to prioritise them.

This is why the Aristotelian approach gives such emphasis to the circumstances or context in trying to judge the morality of an action. The problem it sees with deontology and utilitarianism is that they devote too much attention either to the action itself, considered in the abstract, or to weighing up the likely consequences. Both actions and consequences are essential to any judgement about the ethics of a line of action, but not in isolation. It is the circumstances that really shape the ethics of an action or decision. So, as the circumstances change, so might our judgement of the ethics involved.

In today's pluralistic and multicultural society there is not necessarily agreement about fundamental values or ethical positions. The attempt of theorists to establish one overarching value or theory, which ought to guide actions, seems to have failed as an adequate response. Utilitarianism founders when we disagree on what counts as the good to be maximised or when we are called to take due account of the rights of minorities. Kant's deontology fails to satisfy those who are not prepared to accept his view of absolutes. Second level principles are very useful indicators of essential considerations in resolving problems in ethics, but they do not, of themselves, offer a total solution. In the ensuing ethical conflict we are left to rely on skills of *wise reasoning*. These are skills which can be learned and 'formed' through experience.

This has meant that some contemporary ethicists are returning to aspects of Aristotelian ethics with a focus on practical judgement (MacIntyre, 1985; Nussbaum, 2000; Solomon, 1993; Deveterre, 1995). While not prepared to take on the historical and cultural baggage of Aristotle, they hope to be able to work towards a consensus in ethics through a form of wise reasoning and practical judgement that takes account of the particular issues in the complexity of their circumstances. Such an approach is unlikely to result in complete agreement, but if the issues are subjected to careful examination and appropriate questions reflected on with an eye to the line of action proposed and its likely outcome, a wise judgement can be made which can be reasonably defended.

The result of such an approach is that we will not achieve black-and-white answers (*either/or*), but judgements on what is a reasonable course of action. This will mean that reasonable people may reasonably disagree with the judgements of others, but the ensuing dialogue should help to clarify the issues further and progress the matter.

Many find it difficult to live with this kind of uncertainty when faced with making a decision, but it seems that in ethical matters, in a pluralistic society, the most we can hope for is an open dialogue where cases can be argued on their merits.

How to think about ethical problems

Numerous business textbooks discuss decision-making and offer a number of different models. These models can be extremely useful as a guide to procedures. Sometimes these models, such as the 'Vroom and Yetton decision tree' (1973), take the form of a detailed structure, with arrows showing lines of procedure and alternatives to follow if one line of reasoning does not lead to a satisfactory outcome. Similar decision trees are presented in many texts on ethics. At times, these models can give the impression that if you put the right question in at the top and go through the steps, you are almost guaranteed to come up with the right conclusion. Ethics is not, however, that straightforward and there is not always a guaranteed right answer.

There are a number of ways of making decisions, either individually or in a group. They have many features in common with decision-making in ethics, but there are some differences that are worth considering. Some decision trees are organised as a checklist of things to do or steps to follow, with the intention of leading, sequentially, to the 'correct' decision. Some of them are presented almost as an algorithm that can be applied to a problem to come up with the 'right' answer. Some fail to take any account of ethical issues and base the decision solely on economic factors. A key feature of ethical decision-making approaches is that they focus on helping us with *how* to think about an ethical problem, rather than teaching us *what* to think. As chapter 6 will illustrate, ethical decision-making is a process involving a number of key steps, but the application of these steps in resolving an ethical problem requires good judgement and wisdom. In other words, the steps help the decision-maker approach and think about the problem in a particular way but cannot determine what the content of the decision will be. This can only be done when the facts and context of the particular problem are considered.

Educational leaders need a strategy to aid them in coming to an appropriate decision about how to act in a given situation. An understanding of ethics can help to apply systematic thinking about values and their application to real situations. Leaders need to ensure that their systematic thinking reflects their core values and ethical standards or viewpoints.

There are, however, two possible barriers to sound ethical judgement. One is in the area of personality development; the other comes from lack of clarity about the nature of ethical inquiry.

A sound understanding of developmental psychology is very helpful in understanding how people *actually* respond ethically and morally (Piaget, 1965; Kohlberg, 1971; Power, Higgins & Kohlberg, 1989; Gilligan, 1982; Turiel, 1983). Developmental psychology has demonstrated that it takes time to grow in our approach to ethical decision-making. Self-centredness and the fulfilment of natural impulses mark early childhood. Later, people tend to focus on obedience to parents, authority or law. Those who progress further attain a more abstract and universal approach to making choices through principles and a sense of justice. Some, it would seem, never reach this more abstract level of thinking and judging.

Piaget (1965) believed that individuals develop and refine their sense of morality through their interpersonal interactions and their struggles to determine fair solutions to issues and dilemmas. Kohlberg (1971) is, of course, renowned for his theory of moral development, which identified the structure of moral reasoning underlying choices of action. His theory was based on six stages of moral reasoning in three levels, each of which denotes a clear development in the moral reasoning of the individual. In the first 'preconventional' level, he claimed that an individual's moral perspective tended to be self-centred and concrete in nature (not too concerned with the perspectives of others). In the second 'conventional' level, individuals modify their self-centred tendencies with an understanding that self-identity needs to be redefined, taking into consideration the norms and conventions of the group, and within the framework of what society identifies as 'right' (greater development of trust, respect, loyalty, gratitude, especially at family, group and later societal levels). In the third 'post-conventional' level, individuals reason based on principles, especially those of ethical fairness, justice and human rights from which moral laws are grounded.

Gilligan (1982), offering a perspective based on her research into women's experiences, argued that a morality of care, empathy and responsibility are essential components of moral reasoning and should replace Kohlberg's (1971) morality of justice and rights. Turiel (1983) presented a modification of Kohlberg's theory in his 'domain theory'. This suggested a distinction between a child's concepts of 'morality', which involves a consideration of the effects their actions can have on the wellbeing of others (e.g. can cause them harm), and those based on social knowledge or social convention (agreed upon and predictable rules for behaviour and interaction), which help ensure smooth functioning social exchanges. Turiel, in other words, suggested that Kohlberg's single developmental framework needs to be expanded to include both moral and social meanings of particular dilemmas, choices and courses of action.

The need for a method

The obstacle to ethical development that concerns us here is the general lack of clarity about how to make ethical judgements. When faced with complex ethical situations, many people just do not know where to start or how to proceed. This is a problem of method, which involves: steps to be taken; questions to be asked; values to be clarified; alternatives to be considered; and decisions to be made. To be consistent and coherent in approaching ethical decision-making, we need to have some method of working with and through the issues that face us.

In critiquing the major theories, each was revealed to have problems in practice. Utilitarianism seems too exclusively concerned with the consequences of the action and its implications for increasing the happiness of the greatest number. There are problems in deciding what 'happiness' may mean in a given situation, in trying to evaluate and prioritise short-term or long-term consequences, and in dealing with the question of the rights or needs of minorities as well as the majority.

Consequences of action are certainly a vital element of ethical consideration, but there are also other issues that need to be taken into account. For example, in decision-making in contemporary organisations, too much emphasis can be placed on economic outcomes without adequate attention to other elements. It is a criticism of economic rationalism that the bottom line may become the sole determinant of what ought to be done.

Deontology, with its focus on the nature of the action involved and the absoluteness of its terms of judgement, also appears deficient. The notions of such things as killing, violating rights, truth telling or lying, and keeping promises are essential in our evaluation of the ethics involved; but there are also other things that need to be taken into account. Who performs the action, or is responsible for an omission, in what circumstances and with what knowledge and understanding and under what pressures, must come into our assessment as well. The circumstances surrounding an action also play a vital part in shaping the ethical decision.

The approach of principlism has tried to step down from the abstraction of theories, but it appears that it does not provide a fully adequate approach either. What principles should be selected, and why? Even if we agree on the relevant principles, it is still possible for these principles to conflict. Sometimes, doing good can involve the simultaneous infliction of harm. Sometimes, the demands of justice seem to outweigh the autonomous wishes of individuals. How do we decide which gets priority? We need some method to help us sort out the conflicts.

One advantage of the Aristotelian approach is that it takes note of the complexity of ethical issues and offers suggestions about the need for rational wisdom and a more detailed consideration of the circumstances involved.

The importance of the application of rational wisdom to complex, tension-filled situations is highlighted time and again in the interviews with leaders in this study. This is true particularly with questions of leadership and responsibility. Taking into consideration a number of the points raised in the discussion in this chapter, a method of decision-making in difficult ethical situations is suggested in the next chapter.

Key ideas for reflection

Educational leaders need to incorporate ethical analysis as part of their thinking and reasoning because ethics is at the core of decision-making in many of the challenging situations they face, such as those discussed in chapters 2 and 3.

Ethical decision-making requires educational leaders to be sensitive to the implications and consequences of particular choices in situations involving tensions. It also requires a knowledge of how to apply different ethical viewpoints in everyday decision-making.

While the different approaches to ethics discussed in this chapter are instructive and can assist in resolving difficult ethical questions, it seems obvious that for most situations characterised by tensions, no single approach will deliver a definitive answer. Each approach has its own limitations. In the end, wise reasoning and practical judgements that can be reasonably defended are required in ethical decision-making.

Discussing ethical issues with other key, relevant stakeholders is usually a wise strategy. However, it must be recognised that ethical dialogue usually reflects a variety of voices, all of whom have a right to be heard and believe they are right. Once we start discussing and debating values, we have to confront the fact that, in a multicultural society, there may be no essential agreement on these values.

Questions for reflection

Revisit the critical incident or case that you described at the end of chapter 3 and try to apply the different ethical approaches described in this chapter to it. Most likely, you will find that no one approach provides you with a complete resolution of the tensions involved.

However, the questions that follow will assist you to see how each approach contributed to your thinking:

- What was the relevance/usefulness of rule-based thinking in the situation?
- What consequences (ends-based thinking) did you consider when examining different choices in the situation?
- In what ways were care and compassion (care-based thinking) considered and for whom?
- To what degree did elements of autonomy, common good and justice (principlism) influence the choices made?
- How did your decision-making process involve the use of wise reasoning and practical judgement (rational wisdom)?

Chapter 6

A method for ethical decision-making

Educational leaders require methods and processes that will assist them to probe 'the ethical depths of each situation that calls for a judgement' (Rebore, 2001, p. 31). They need these methods more than ever before as they enter a period of great change, uncertainty, and ethical relativism. Too few educational leaders today have a background or formal formation in ethical decision-making.

To assist leaders to consider the ethical dimensions of tension situations and make informed and wise choices in such challenging situations as those discussed in chapters 2 and 3, the following ethical decision method is proposed. It is best if such a method is used within a group context so that responsibility for the final solution to an ethical tension is shared. Also, most, if not all, of the steps in the proposed method lend themselves to dialogue and serious discussion among key stakeholders. This is a point that will be more fully developed in chapter 7.

Proposed method for ethical decision-making

To be consistent and coherent in approaching ethical decision-making, educational leaders need to have some method of working with and through the issues that face them. Making ethical judgements when facing complex ethical situations is hard enough already, without adding the problem of not knowing where to start or how to proceed. The following ten steps will help leaders to make more effective decisions in situations of ethical tension:

1 Determine the nature of the situation.
2 Clarify the facts.

3 Identify the players.
4 Think of several options for action.
5 Evaluate options using different ethical approaches.
6 Choose the best option.
7 Explain your choice.
8 Work out how to implement the option.
9 Take action carefully.
10 Reflect and learn.

Each step is explored in more detail below.

Step 1: Determine the nature of the situation

Does it constitute a conundrum between right-and-right, a dilemma between wrong-and-wrong, or a moral temptation between right-and-wrong? What 'contestable values dualities' are involved? (See discussion in chapters 3, 4 and 5 and framework for analysis of tensions in chapter 4.)

Step 2: Clarify the facts

As stated in chapter 5, good ethical decision-making relies on a thorough collection and understanding of the facts. Remember that assumptions (including your own) and hearsay are not the same as facts. Also, there may be disagreements about the meaning of the facts of the case. (See the discussion later in this chapter.)

No amount of careful reasoning will rescue a judgement based on erroneous information. There is sometimes a danger in ethical discussion that we can get involved in an argument on some issue without fully understanding what the issue is all about. Just listen to some staffroom or dinner table discussions about controversial issues like the cloning of animals or humans, stem cell research or the use of the drug RU486 and then reflect on how well the various speakers really understand the issues. In other words, we may get involved in debate without an adequate knowledge or understanding of the facts.

One of the most important things about making an ethical decision on complex issues, like those discussed in chapter 3 on tensions, is to begin with a thorough understanding of the facts. Sometimes this will require some research to find out what is really at the heart of the issue. As was made clear in the case cited earlier on the purported use of drugs by girls in a school, the facts of the case were in dispute. In real-life situations the facts are often hard to determine; different people will have their own versions of them and may also interpret them differently. For the educational leader who has to make a decision in such uncertain and contested circumstances, it is necessary to understand the reality of the situation to the best of his/her ability.

A key point in any effective method for decision-making in ethics is to get as much knowledge as possible of the whole issue. This involves not only the particular issue in question, but a series of other points that will help to understand this reality. It is necessary to know: what the issue is; who the central players are; why they might be involved; what their interests might be; what alternatives there might be; and what the outcomes of those alternatives are likely to be. These are what Aristotle would have called the circumstances of the act. Without knowledge of these one can hardly be said to have a grip on the facts of the issue.

Sometimes it is just one of these factors which might alter the ethical evaluation of the tension. For instance, *who* does the action could be quite significant.

Step 3: Identify the players

See if you can determine the intentions and interests of the key players, especially those with a stake in particular potential outcomes. You may also need to be aware of the peripheral players in the situation to select the best action or implement it most effectively.

You may need to consider the appropriateness of actions in the context of who did, does or will do them. An important educational decision ought to be made by the 'correct' person or people, with the relevant information, appropriate authority and expertise. In the case cited in chapter 2 of the young boy who attacked another boy, kicking him, it is an important fact that the attacker had been diagnosed with a medical problem and was on medication. It would seem sensible to involve this boy's doctor in any decisions on his future. In this case parents and teachers got emotionally involved and took sides. Some were considerate of the boy's medical condition while others were adamant that the aggressive behaviour required the boy's removal from the school. The wise course of action would be to engage in dialogue with a number of key stakeholders, try to establish some common ground, and draw on the wisdom of the group for the decision.

Motivation, or the intention underlying the action or decision, is also important in helping to evaluate the ethics involved. Sometimes this is quite difficult, since it is often impossible to know why people act or decide in the manner they do. Educational leaders need to get to know the people they work with, especially what normally motivates them. A teacher who constantly acts in the interests of students, for example, is likely to be acting from this value position with regard to any particular decision. The important point here is that the ethical reality may not be adequately addressed by the simple description of the action involved. In other words, our understanding of the ethical tensions and realities of a particular situation will be assisted by a better knowledge and understanding of the people involved.

Step 4: Think of several options for action

When trying to come to grips with the full reality of an ethical issue, educational leaders also need to check whether there are viable options or alternatives. The same end may be achievable by less harmful or intrusive means, for example, an offer of voluntary redundancies rather than mass sacking. Consider multiple ways to resolve the situation, and the likely consequences of each. You will need, of course, to consider any legal and/or regulatory codes or constraints as well.

It is important to ask, 'Is the proposed action the only way to handle the situation?' Thinking seriously about alternatives and their possible consequences can help ensure that narrowly-based solutions are avoided. For example, in the case in chapter 3 involving a 'disadvantaged student' who had received a 'blue slip' for misbehaviour, the principal and the executive considered different alternative solutions to the problem. The problem was:

> . . . if a student has received more than one 'blue slip', that student is not allowed to participate in special activities such as excursions, visits or play sports until his/her behaviour has improved. If it is their (sic) first 'blue slip', the ban is for one week only. One student,

who is a talented athlete, had reached eligibility to participate at regional level. The student had received no support from home and has been known to run in bare feet! One week prior to the athletic event he earned, fairly, his first 'blue slip'. Technically the full week was up the day after the carnival. The dilemma of allowing this child a chance at the carnival was taken to the Executive who decided he should participate.

Although the specific alternatives are not described by the principal in this case, the executive most likely canvassed a number of alternatives and weighed up their consequences. The principal suggested that they considered the possible longer-term consequences for the student if he were banned from competing in the sports event at which he excelled and that it was 'a once-in-a-lifetime opportunity for the student'. He also stated that executive members were clear that choosing to allow the student to compete set an uncomfortable precedent, and that other students and their parents might query its fairness, because other students in similar circumstances had in the past been prohibited from participating in similar events.

The principal in this case decided to discuss the possible alternatives and the solution of the problem with his executive group. Given the complexity of the challenges and tensions discussed in chapters 2 and 3, sharing the responsibility for their resolution seems like a sensible approach. In fact, a strong trend emerging in educational systems and schools is for educational leaders to share their leadership responsibilities with other key stakeholders. In the next chapter, I will argue that it is an ethical imperative for formal leaders to share the burdens and responsibilities as well as the satisfaction and excitement of leading their school communities.

Step 5: Evaluate options using different ethical approaches

For detail on some of the major ethical approaches to consider, see the discussion in chapter 5. A brief summary follows below:

- Deontological or rules-based approach would suggest that in choosing an option we should do our moral duty through rational reflection.
- Utilitarian approach would suggest that the option should produce the greatest balance of benefits over harm.

- Care-based approach would suggest that we primarily follow our duty of care as a fellow human being and a professional educator.
- Princiciplism approach would suggest that the option should, as far as possible, enable people to make the decisions that are rightfully theirs, contribute to the greater good of the community while minimising harm to individuals, and treat people justly.
- Rational wisdom approach would suggest that the decision should be based on wise reasoning combined with practical judgement, or a 'wisdom way of knowing', and exhibit those virtues that reflect human beings at their best and therefore lead to the living of a 'good life'.

In many of the tensions discussed in chapter 3, principals were concerned with consequences of their decisions and actions for both individuals and groups. The consequences of decisions and actions are an important consideration. No one can say they have captured the full reality involved in choosing an option or making a decision until they have examined the foreseeable consequences. Educational leaders are ethically responsible for those under their care and it is ethically unacceptable to ignore the reasonably foreseeable consequences of an option or decision. There may well, of course, be consequences that are beyond their foresight and control.

There were definite consequences, some foreseen and others unforeseen, in the case in chapter 3 where the grandfather spoke to his granddaughter at school with the principal's permission and then arranged to pick her up from the park on the Saturday and take her to her aunt's house. The principal had information that the girl's mother, a single parent, was having a problem with drugs and that the girl was increasingly being neglected by her mother. The primary concern was that if no action were taken the consequences for the girl would be very negative. This is why he allowed the grandfather to speak directly to his granddaughter even though the rules stated clearly that only the mother had such direct access. The principal was aware that the consequences could be very negative for him if the mother made a formal complaint to the proper authorities. The unforeseen consequence for the principal in allowing the grandfather to speak on the phone to his granddaughter was that he arranged to pick her up from the park and, without her mother's permission, take her to her aunt's place where he knew the girl would be well cared for. In a strictly legal sense, this constituted kidnapping and the principal, unwittingly, was party to it.

In the end, the mother accepted the action that had been taken and no negative consequences eventuated. The principal regretted his decision even though it had a positive outcome. He stated:

> No action was taken against anyone, and all parties are happy with the new situation. But I don't think that I can judge my actions purely on the basis of the final outcome. As a leader, I should have been able to work within the guidelines to bring about a favourable result. I think I showed inexperience. I was fortunate that the repercussions of my actions, and inactions, were positive. If I were faced with the same situation in the future, I would hope that I would handle the situation with a much greater sense of professionalism. In fact, I am confident that I would handle the situation differently.

Step 6: Choose the best option

This will be the option that best caters for the values and ethical standards you believe to be important. *Both/and* thinking is recommended. Remember you need to exercise good judgement based on a well-considered reasoning process and on defensible ethical standards or principles.

Struggling to come to grips with the full reality of a tension situation in order to make some detailed evaluation of it will place educational leaders in a better position to reach an informed ethical decision. The judgement reached may be a certain and confident one, but it will sometimes be tentative and open to revision. A tentative judgement may, in the particular circumstances of a case, be the best that can be managed. Through no fault of their own, leaders often do not have a mastery of all the facts and may not be able to foresee all the consequences, but they have to make a decision anyway. While mistakes of judgement will inevitably be made, if leaders are confident that they have done their best to work through the issue in a thorough manner, then it can be argued that they have done all that can be demanded from an ethical point of view.

Differences of ethical judgement can, however, become a problem when it comes to decisions where there are irreconcilable differences of opinion in a group situation. If it is a matter of a group decision and unanimity is not possible, then some form of integrity-preserving compromise will need to be reached. Some people are immediately troubled when they hear of compromise in ethical matters. It can seem to be the abandonment of principle for the sake of group cohesion and harmony. Accusations of abandonment of principle can be extremely troubling to conscientious individuals. It may, in fact, be seen by some as a failure of integrity.

It seems, nonetheless, that there can be such a thing as *integrity-preserving compromise*. Compromising in situations of ethical complexity is, according to Benjamin (1990, p. 121) more 'the outcome of reflective judgement than of a rationalistic decision procedure'. Key values guiding the exercise of such reflective judgement are 'individual integrity, overall utility . . . and equal respect' (p. 122). Benjamin thus ties the notion of integrity in with both utilitarian and deontological values. He admits that these notions of individual integrity, overall welfare, and mutual respect are imprecise, and that individuals and groups may differ in their interpretation of them.

With creative imagination and the desire to obtain the best practical outcome in a complex situation, a reasonable compromise can sometimes be reached. It will, however, require some relinquishment of one's views and values. At times, an individual will be able to do this in the search for the overall good, but, at other times, the sacrifice of values will be too great, and some may be unable to compromise on particular values of personal importance.

The principal who decided, in the case in chapter 3, to support the redundancy application of a staff member even though he believed that a dismissal process was a more appropriate option was opting for a reasonable compromise. He had concluded that with dismissal being a prolonged and time-consuming process he could see his time used more productively. He stated:

> I weighed up the time and effort involved in trying to bring an unwilling and uncommitted staff member up to speed against the other priorities I had, together with the emerging initiatives and projects which were in the planning stage. I also thought very

carefully about where my time would be better spent in terms of staff development, change management, redirecting the organisational culture and re-positioning the school for the future. I also know what it is like to prove incompetence in the area I work in. I believe I made the right choice.

Obviously, the principal in this case considered at least two, if not more, alternatives.

Step 7: Explain your choice

Demonstrate to yourself or others why you have chosen this option and why it is a better resolution of the issue than the other options – reflect on how you would defend it publicly. It is a good idea to document your thoughts as an aid to memory. Verbalising and writing down your justification, especially if it is a decision of considerable import, will assist you to see any gaps in your reasoning and will give you an opportunity to receive constructive criticism from others.

Step 8: Work out how to implement the option

Sometimes the devil is in the detail. What will make this option work? What might undermine it? Who will you need to engage in the implementation to get ownership of the option? Develop a well-thought-out plan for taking appropriate action and anticipate possible obstacles or bottlenecks. As with any change process, open dialogue and collaboration with those who are responsible for implementing the option is essential. Many excellent decisions have failed at the implementation stage because of poor planning or because key personnel were not invited to participate in their implementation.

Step 9: Take action carefully

If the action taken involves a change in people's behaviours, then special care must be taken to ensure that their anxieties and fears are considered and addressed. Don't ever underestimate the trauma that some go through when they are required to change long-formed habits and behaviours. Look for honest feedback and keep an open mind. Modify the implementation processes if they are causing harm or having an unreasonable impact on the people involved. Also, be prepared to change the decision if new facts or unexpected consequences come to light. There will, of course, be times when the decision has to be implemented or the action taken in the interests of the common good even if some of those affected are opposed. In the end, good judgement is required in such situations.

Step 10: Reflect and learn

Make sure you critically reflect on the whole process and its outcomes, and note what you have learned from it. Reflection and feedback are essential components of any effective learning process and should occur throughout the decision processes. It is also important to apply this learning to improve or refine your decision-making for the future, taking into consideration the particular context in which you lead.

Additional considerations on this method

This may seem like a daunting set of steps, but most wise educational leaders already operate this way. They may not follow each step in detail, but they flash through the thought processes quickly – after all, thought travels much faster than the speed of light. Applying the steps should become a habit of mind. While the method may be perceived by some as too time-consuming, without such a considered approach much more time can be wasted picking up the pieces after a disastrous decision.

There are a number of other considerations that can guide educational leaders when trying to make an ethical evaluation of a particular tension. Factors such as their own feelings or past experiences can be quite useful. Feelings can easily prejudice judgement, but they can also be a good, almost instinctive, guide to right and wrong. An immediate feeling of rejection or revulsion for a proposed line of action should at least give pause, and suggest that the whole issue needs closer examination. In the case of the students in chapter 3, who were asked by the teacher to enter other students' marks into a computer, one of the girls instinctively felt that it was wrong and checked her concern with her father who recommended that she discuss the issue with the principal. If educational leaders instinctively feel that a decision about downsizing, or expulsion of a student, is unjust, then it may well be worth searching to see if there are other alternatives. If past experience, either their own or that of others, suggests that a certain decision will cause more harm than good, then leaders should at least reconsider.

Ethical principles and careful attention to reasoning and argument help us in our evaluation process. No simple application of principles, like a template, to a problem will resolve the issue, but basic principles of justice, fair play and human decency are likely to help us make a more balanced and just evaluation and decision. We need to think through the issues and work with them, not just opt for a simplistic solution. As indicated earlier, leadership involves the application of a 'wisdom way of knowing', a rational wisdom, to complex and contested situations.

In the end, the resolution of complex multidimensional situations requires the use of good judgement based on a sound knowledge of the facts of the case and an understanding of ethical theories and principles.

The laws and customs of our society can also serve to guide decision-making. These may not be designed for simple application, but they are worthy of consideration and care to see if, and to what extent, they may have implications for the final decision. Leaders must remember, however, that laws or system regulations may not be the final word in discussing the ethics of an option or decision. Their implications must at least be examined, and educational leaders must realise that if they break laws or go against guidelines in the search for a higher ethical value, then they are liable to bear the consequences for that action. There may be circumstances in which violation of the letter of the law may be justified (such as the case where the principal allowed the grandfather to speak with his granddaughter) but one ought to proceed with extreme caution and an awareness of the likely consequences.

Key ideas for reflection

In situations involving ethical tensions, educational leaders need a method for making decisions about them. They need to know, among other things discussed in this chapter: what the issue is – whether it is an ethical one; who the central players are and their possible interests, motives and intentions; what alternatives there might be and their likely consequences; and what the best outcomes could be, especially as they relate to the common good.

In some instances, they may have to settle for 'integrity-preserving compromise', even though this might be regarded by some as abandonment of principle and relinquishment of their values. Compromise can be seen as 'sitting on the fence' or worse 'selling one's soul' for the sake of group harmony and cohesion. It can also be regarded as ethical relativism or as lacking moral courage. Compromises can be all these things, which is why it is so important to compromise only when such a compromise preserves integrity. Compromise should only be entered into after due and careful consideration of other values-driven alternatives.

Questions for reflection

In the case cited earlier in this chapter on the principal's decision to compromise by supporting an application for a voluntary redundancy package when he personally believed that initiating a dismissal process was the 'right' option, reflect on the following questions:

- Was this compromise justified, in your opinion?
- What might other key stakeholders think of his compromise?
- What have you done in similar situations?
- What advice would you give to a new principal, if and when he/she had to deal with a similar situation?

Chapter 7

Shared and distributed
leadership in schools

Schools need to think differently about the quality and depth of their leadership if they are to respond effectively to the types of challenges and tensions discussed in chapters 2 and 3. Many educational leaders leave themselves isolated and alone, taking primary responsibility for the leadership of their school. This constitutes a very narrow view of leadership and ignores the leadership talents of teachers, students and other community stakeholders. As was suggested in chapter 6 when introducing the proposed method for ethical decision-making, it is wise for any formal educational leader, such as a school principal, to tap into the expertise and wisdom of his/her colleagues when attempting to resolve contentious challenges and tensions. Sharing the responsibility for making decisions in such situations will also help generate greater ownership of the decisions.

Another reason for engaging in dialogue with others and inviting them to share in decision-making is, according to Surowiecki (2005, p. 29), that diversity matters and there is wisdom in the 'crowd'. He argues that diversity of people and their information helps in coming to a better decision or resolution because it actually adds perspectives that would be absent if the decision is made by one person, even by an expert, and because it takes away, or at least weakens, some of the destructive characteristics of group decision-making, for example, 'group think'. Surowiecki concludes that diverse groups of individuals 'will make better and more robust forecasts and more intelligent decisions than a skilled decision-maker', but that 'groups that are too much alike find it harder to keep learning, because each member is bringing less and less new information to the table . . . and they become progressively less able to investigate alternatives' (p. 31). Grouping only smart people (experts) together also doesn't work that well, because they tend to resemble each other in what they can do. He concludes that it is better to entrust a diverse group 'with varying degrees of knowledge and insight' with major decisions 'rather than leaving them in the hands of one or two people, no matter how smart those people are' (p. 31). He encourages leaders, when making decisions, to engage with others who have different knowledge bases and perspectives because 'the simple fact of making a group diverse makes it better at problem solving' (p. 30).

It would be advisable for a principal engaged in the steps of ethical decision-making discussed in chapter 6 to engage in dialogue with other key stakeholders. It would seem essential to listen to diverse viewpoints when attempting to: determine the ethical tensions; clarify the facts; determine possible options and their likely consequences; choose specific solutions, explain and implement them; see the action through, evaluating its impact; and learn from the experience.

There would seem to be a need, therefore, for a shift in the meaning and practices of educational leadership in many schools, especially those where the principal prefers to make decisions on her/his own. To enhance leadership of schools, educational leaders and educational communities need to rethink what educational leadership actually means and involves – its definition, purpose, scope and processes as well as its practices.

What is proposed here is the building of organisational cultures that promote and support greater sharing and distribution of leadership in schools. Such cultures help enhance professional dialogue between and among diverse groups of stakeholders, and promote an environment where leadership and decision-making are seen as a collective responsibility and where sharing is the norm.

Sharing leadership

Educational leaders need to create sharing cultures where others willingly participate in and are rewarded for the successful performance of their leadership responsibilities. Such sharing is not merely a matter of splitting or distributing tasks and responsibilities in a task-oriented approach, it requires a mindset shift. It requires a 'letting go', especially by principals who have been used to leading from the front. For this to happen, educational leaders need to be secure enough in their own identity to freely share and distribute what were previously 'their' responsibilities. This, as we shall see in chapter 9, requires authenticity on the part of those in leadership positions. Authenticity and genuinely shared leadership, in turn, provide excellent modelling for students of healthy, communal ways of living.

A contemporary view is that leadership in a complex organisation, such as a school, requires the energy, commitment and contributions of all who work there. From this perspective, shared leadership is a product of the ongoing processes of interaction and negotiation amongst all school members as they construct and reconstruct a reality of working productively and compassionately together each day. Leadership, therefore, can be viewed as a shared communal phenomenon derived from the interactions and relationships of groups. The quality of relationships greatly influences everything else that happens in organisations, including the quality and impact of leadership (Duignan & Bhindi, 1997, p. 201).

As well as relationships, deeply held and unquestioned concepts influence what happens in organisations. Sharing leadership requires all the key stakeholders in a school community to rethink what constitutes leadership. Assumptions that underpin leadership – such as those underpinning power, authority, influence, position, status, responsibility and accountability, as well as personal and professional relationships – need to be identified, critiqued and adjusted as necessary.

Often leadership is equated with formal roles, and this mindset can prove an obstacle to sharing. In some hierarchical organisations, leaders expect decisions to be accepted because of their role or rank and they are surprised when their colleagues will neither follow a poor decision, nor explain why they think it was not a good decision. Leadership in such circumstances can be seen as based on the authority or power given by position. This hierarchical view limits an understanding of the need for all members to show leadership, when and where appropriate. Those in formal leadership positions need to let go of the idea that leadership is hierarchically distributed and embrace the idea that it is their responsibility to develop and nurture leadership in others.

Most successful sports teams have what is referred to as 'depth on the bench': sometimes their key players, their on-field leaders, get injured, but the reserves waiting on the bench have the capability to step into the breach. Organisations, too, need reserves of leadership if they are to be successful in the longer term. These leaders, of course, should not be on the bench but in the game, participating with skill, commitment and enthusiasm. A benefit in having depth of leadership in an organisation is that it creates a larger and deeper pool of leaders from which future executives and middle managers can be selected. A first key step in creating this depth of leadership is to share leadership responsibilities with others.

A commitment to sharing responsibility for leadership in schools often grows out of the shared vision, beliefs and efforts of a committed group of teachers, administrators, support staff, and parents who have a sense of belonging, a sense of being valued members of their organisation and a deep commitment to collective action for whole-school success (Crowther *et al.* 2002a). Ideally, all staff members, including newly arrived staff, would have a clear picture of their special space in the leadership framework of their school. If the depth of leadership in the organisation is to be enhanced, they must feel that they are valued as significant contributors to the leadership of their organisation, no matter at what level or in what area.

While much is written and spoken about the need for shared and distributed leadership in schools, the characteristics, the context, and obstacles to its more complete implementation need to be explored and understood. The language of contemporary leadership is often replete with the jargon of sharing and collaboration (e.g. inclusivity; caring; collaborative decision-making; empowerment of followers; shared vision and goals), but frequently the language constitutes a rhetoric that is never fully realised. There is little doubt that the evolving complexity and uncertainty of life and work in schools compels educational leaders to work more collaboratively with a growing number of people. It is time to make the rhetoric a reality, and create collaborative communities that can embrace uncertainty and paradox.

Teachers as leaders

The concept of teachers as leaders has been the subject of increasing research over recent years. In some contexts, it has been linked to the question of whether teaching has gained recognition and acceptance as a profession (Institute for Educational Leadership, 2001, p. 6). Recent research points to the central role of teachers in influencing student performance and outcomes in schooling (Andrews *et al.* 2000; Crowther *et al.* 2002a & 2002b; Darling-Hammond, 1999).

Andrews *et al.* (2002, p. 25) developed a 'teachers as leaders' framework that highlights the importance of two key factors: teachers' values with regard to enhancing teaching and learning; and the capacity of teachers to create new meanings, especially for students, in the learning process. They make an important distinction between teachers as leaders in a specialised area such as pedagogy and discipline (e.g. subject leadership) and leadership that contributes to whole-school reform and improvement. In other words, while teachers should focus, primarily, on leading improvement in pedagogy and curriculum, it is best if this is done as a whole-school initiative. The principal is in the best position to ensure that this larger school orientation is achieved.

This focus on school improvement was central to a recent Federal Government trial project of a shared leadership approach in schools in Australia (Chesterton & Duignan, 2004). The project, entitled the 'IDEAS Project', included a philosophy and framework based on the concept of 'parallel leadership', which encourages teachers to take on leadership responsibilities for curriculum and pedagogy, 'in parallel' with the principal and the executive, but within a whole-school improvement framework (Crowther *et al.* 2002a & 2002b). This involves teachers working together in teams across grades and subjects in order to overcome their often isolationist habits and practices. It also places their leadership of curriculum and pedagogy within the larger vision and purpose of the school as a whole.

Crowther *et al.*'s work is the most influential in the growing body of literature that supports various approaches to shared leadership. In their view, teachers should be actively engaged in decisions about learning and teaching. Of course, students, parents and the community are also stakeholders and, as such, should have an input into such decisions, but teachers, as educational professionals, must be in the front line in determining the nature and content of curriculum and the approaches to and processes of pedagogy, learning and teaching.

For contemporary educational leaders to develop and foster the growth of shared leadership in their schools, they need to help teachers to develop collaborative and shared mental models and meanings that bind them together as a learning community. The key emphasis is on learning together, sharing and creating processes and conditions that encourage everyone in the school community to learn, grow, and be creative together. This is, in essence, what is meant by sharing leadership in a school community. Sharing leadership, in the context of the school as a learning community, involves growing, nurturing and supporting competent and capable teachers to become key leaders, especially of curriculum and pedagogy.

However, a key argument in a shared approach to leadership is that it needs to be widely distributed across key stakeholders, not just teachers. A number of researchers have explored the nature and structure of what they refer to as 'distributed leadership' (Pearce & Sims, 2002; Harris, 2002; Spillane, Halverson & Diamond, 2001; and Elmore, 2000).

Distributing leadership

Pearce and Sims (2002, p. 188) reported on a study that analysed the behaviour of appointed team leaders (vertical leadership) *versus* the distributed influence and effectiveness of those within the team (distributed leadership). Distributed leadership, they concluded, accounted for much of the effectiveness of change management teams. In another research project on leadership in schools, which took leadership practice as the unit of analysis, the researchers concluded that a distributed approach to leadership can improve practice by making leadership in the school more transparent. It enables the ways in which teachers and other leaders think and act to change teaching and learning to be seen more clearly. Such an approach to leadership, they suggested, can help teachers and educational leaders 'identify dimensions of their practice, articulate relations among these dimensions, and think about changing their practice' (Spillane *et al.* 2001, p. 24).

Leadership of schools is beyond the capacity of any one person, or of those in formal leadership positions only, and should be distributed to engage the 'contours of expertise' in the school community, creating a culture that provides coherence, guidance and direction for teaching, learning and leadership (Elmore, 2000, p. 15). Contours of expertise suggest that there are rich veins of expertise to be found throughout organisations for those who know the organisational terrain well. Distributed leadership is, however, more than collaboration among teachers. Collaborative work by teachers will not by itself lead to changed teacher practices and improved learning outcomes. To engage teachers productively in leadership there must be a whole-school focus on change and improvement, a larger purpose than just collaboration for its own sake.

Distributed leadership, therefore, must have a clear purpose and focus to bring about whole-school improvement in learning and teaching. In this way, distributing leadership can be an important motivator and a contributor to the quality of teaching and learning in the school and in the classroom. Of course, collaboration and teamwork must occur between and among teachers and these collegial relationships should empower them to make key decisions on pedagogy and learning (Silins & Mulford, 2002) and be grounded in 'mutual trust, support and enquiry' (Harris, 2000, p. 3).

However, it would seem that distributed leadership is not easy to establish and maintain in practice, and consequently is not a predominant characteristic of many contemporary schools. A traditional emphasis in schools on privacy, individualism and 'idiosyncratic institutional practice' makes collective action difficult (Harris, 2002, p. 7). These barriers must be breached if genuine distribution of leadership is to occur. If, as has already been suggested, leadership for school improvement cannot be the responsibility of one or even a few people then it seems reasonable to conclude that a key challenge is to find ways of enabling more teachers to become leaders and supporting them as necessary to change current pedagogical, teaching and learning practices. A new paradigm of the teaching profession is needed, one that recognises both the capacity of the profession to provide desperately needed school revitalisation and the striking potential of teachers to provide new forms of leadership in schools and communities (Crowther *et al.* 2002b).

While participation of teachers is a key ingredient of true distributed leadership, the school principal has an important role to perform. A recent review of an Australian Federal Government trial of a shared, distributed model of leadership in schools identified the principal as a key to its success (Chesterton & Duignan, 2004). The principal has to have the capacity to share leadership, to 'let go' so that teachers' voices can be heard in key decisions not only on teaching and learning but also on whole-school improvement. Principals with traditional views of position, power and hierarchical structures may find themselves unable to 'unfreeze' their habitual ways of thinking, doing and organising. Principals need to develop their leadership capabilities if they are to feel comfortable in engaging fully with teachers in shared or distributed leadership (Duignan & Marks, 2003).

Based on a substantial research agenda, The National College for School Leadership (NCSL) in England (2004) proposed five pillars of distributed leadership in schools:

1 **Self-confident and self-effacing headship** – a desire to make an impact upon the world without a strong need for personal status;
2 **Clarity of structure and accountability** – defining responsibilities to create 'permission to act';
3 **Investment in leadership capability** – to build the value, beliefs and attributes of effective leadership in all members of staff;
4 **A culture of trust** – to facilitate boldness, debate and co-operation; and
5 **A turning point** – specific actions and events in a school's history that lend momentum to the evolution of distributed leadership (NCSL, 2006, pp. 21–32).

While all five pillars are important, investment in leadership capability (number three) is one of the most urgent in the Australian educational systems and is the focus of the next chapter. The question that arises for me is the degree to which many educational leaders are capable of responding effectively to the challenges and tensions already discussed in this book, especially those with ethical implications for their schools. In the next chapter, I argue that educational leaders will need, first and foremost, to be capable human beings, as well as knowledgeable and competent professionals, in order to cope with the types of challenges and tensions discussed in this book.

Key ideas for reflection

One key way to enhance leadership capacity in schools is to rethink what educational leadership actually means and involves – its definition, purpose, scope and processes as well as its content. In many schools, there is a need for a shift in the meaning, perspective and scope of educational leadership to promote and support greater sharing and distribution of leadership responsibilities.

A shared approach to leadership can enhance professional dialogue and create an environment where core educational and pedagogical decisions are seen as a collective professional responsibility. A distributed approach to leadership identifies the contours of expertise within the school community and harnesses the talents of all key stakeholders for the purpose of improving the processes, content and outcomes of teaching and learning.

While the need for shared and distributed leadership in schools appears to be well understood, the obstacles to its implementation need to be explored and better understood. Educational leaders have the challenge of creating conditions in which the key school community stakeholders are willing and able to collaborate, channelling all efforts towards achieving the shared vision and goals of the school community.

Teachers, especially, need to trust and support one another in a shared working environment in order to optimise learning opportunities and outcomes for all students. However, many teachers may have to overcome a culture of individualism, privacy, professional isolationism and idiosyncratic institutional practices. Research indicates that for teachers to share in the leadership of curriculum and pedagogy, there needs to be a focus on whole-school improvement in learning and teaching as opposed to piece-meal change in a department or subject area. Engaging teachers in shared and distributed leadership can be an important motivator and contributor to the quality of teaching and learning throughout the school. Collegial collaboration and teamwork among teachers should empower them to make significant and influential improvements in teaching, pedagogy and learning.

For schools with closed professional cultures, shared and distributed leadership will not come about just because literature recommends it or because some school stakeholders 'talk it up' as a good idea. Changes in attitudes and mindsets are necessary before changes in practices can occur. A useful starting point, perhaps a turning point, is to encourage discussion and dialogue about the assumptions that underpin sharing and distributing leadership, as well as the strategies and actions necessary to achieve such change.

Questions for reflection

Reflection 1 – assumptions and concepts

- What assumptions underpin a shared or distributed approach to leadership?
- Can leadership actually be shared and/or distributed? Remember that leadership is, essentially, an influencing process. Can influence be shared and/or distributed?
- How about power? Authority? Responsibility? Accountability? Can they be shared and/or distributed?
- What changes to position, status and personal and professional relationships might be brought about by sharing or distributing leadership?

Reflection 2 – case study

Reflect on a recent project or event where effective sharing of the leadership occurred:

- What were the key reasons for this successful sharing?
- What lessons did you learn for sharing and distributing leadership in the future?

Reflection 3 – getting started
- How can cultures of shared/distributed leadership be better promoted and supported in schools?
- What assumptions and mindsets need to be challenged?
- What positive steps can be taken, almost immediately?
- What needs to happen to sustain such cultures of shared leadership?

Chapter 8

Why we need capable educational leaders

The discussion in chapter 1 pointed out that education systems and schools are constantly changing to adapt to pressure from the globalisation of technology, information and knowledge. As well, the discussion in chapters 2 and 3 highlighted the nature of the challenges and tensions facing many contemporary educational leaders. A key point in this chapter is that educational leaders need to develop their leadership capabilities if they hope to lead wisely, effectively and ethically in uncertain times.

Educational leaders, to be credible, have to be capable human beings as well as capable professional educators. They will need to be good managers and efficient, competent and productive practitioners but they must also be capable human beings because 'it is not a matter of knowing something, but becoming someone, not just a matter of knowing relevant things, but of becoming a relevant person' (Kelly, 2000, p. 19).

To be capable as human beings and as educators, educational leaders must use their knowledge, skills and competencies confidently, with good judgement and wisdom, in challenging and rapidly changing circumstances. The development of wisdom and good judgement cannot only be dependent upon competency training and development, which is currently the case for educational leaders, especially principals, in many education systems. It is argued in this chapter that knowledge acquisition and training in competencies may be inadequate as a basis for developing educational leaders for the future.

The problems with competency

There is considerable critique in the literature of competency-based models of leadership development. Critics question the possibility of fragmenting leadership into key result areas, competencies and performance indicators (Kaplan & Norton, 1996; Onsman, 2003; Duignan & Marks, 2003). They object to generic checklists that separate the performance from the context within which development occurs. They point to difficulties associated with making professional judgements and leadership development decisions based on checklists or performance indicators that encourage black-and-white thinking and decision-making.

Principals in this study expressed concern that important aspects of leadership were ignored in a competency-based approach because they were just too hard to specify and measure. As a way forward, these participants recommended that leadership development programs should identify key dimensions of leadership in a particular context, i.e. categories and descriptions of leadership responsibilities and the knowledge, skills, attitudes, qualities and wisdom (here referred to as 'capabilities') that were needed to be successful in leadership. They regarded competency-based models as too narrow and simplistic. Some of their comments provide insights into their concerns: 'there is no one formula for leadership'; 'leadership is just too dynamic, situational and unpredictable to be highly specified in this way'. They also felt that the fragmentation of their role into key result areas, competencies and performance indicators was artificial.

Recent research amongst school principals in NSW indicated that over the last ten years competency-based training on skills and knowledge accounted for 87% of all professional development activities for principals. Such an approach, principals suggested, prepared them for conditions of stability and certainty that no longer exist in most schools (Marks, 2002–03).

Despite the general desire of school leaders to demonstrate the type of educational leadership discussed in chapter 1 (visionary, authentic, ethical, strategic, people-centred and motivational), principals in New South Wales (NSW) reported that competencies relating to legal and regulatory compliance issues (e.g. occupational health and safety; child protection; cleaning and maintenance contracts) dominated their day-to-day practices. Because of the increasingly diverse and seemingly endless compliance-style expectations for the role associated with the devolution-agenda of the 1990s, principals are focusing on the 'management of compliance issues' at the expense of 'shared educational leadership' (Marks, 2002–03). This then becomes the role model for aspiring leaders. What younger teachers and middle executives are observing is the principal acting primarily as the 'site manager'.

It would appear from Marks' research, as well as from further work on effective leadership preparation programs, that many principals have not been able to focus on the development of their personal and professional leadership capabilities (Marks, 2003). Aspiring principals, similarly, have not been focusing on developing their leadership capabilities as these have not been modelled by incumbent principals; have not been part of leadership preparation programs; are rarely included in the criteria for merit selection; and therefore are not perceived as being valued by employing authorities. Yet recent researchers strongly suggest that it is the personal, interpersonal and social leadership capabilities that make the difference in the effective leadership of schools (Goleman *et al.* 2003; Stephenson, 2000; Hargreaves & Fullan, 1998; Begley & Johansson, 2002). In fact, the findings from research with middle executives (the pool for future leaders) in a number of NSW schools highlight two very significant conclusions:

1 The principal, as the role model for leadership, is seen as someone who is usually preoccupied with policy, rules and regulation compliance and is therefore not the 'educational leader'. Personal and interpersonal capabilities – such as calmness, reliability, trust, confidence, wisdom, tolerance, self-awareness, social awareness, self-reflection and empathy – are often overwhelmed by the managerial demands of the moment. Principals overall present an image of being frustrated, harassed, or stressed, with low job-satisfaction levels.

2 The training and development offered to, and often mandated for, principals and/or middle-level school leaders is dominated by regulation and legal/policy compliance issues. There are few

programs offered for the development of personal and interpersonal skills, emotional intelligences, cultural and strategic leadership, leadership of change, implementing mentoring or coaching, developing shared leadership, or growing leadership capacity in self and in others (Marks, 2002–03).

The message, as perceived by many middle-level leaders and younger teachers, seems to be that leadership capabilities are not valued in their systems and schools. Simultaneously, a significantly lower number of suitably qualified middle-level educational leaders are applying for the principalship (d'Arbon, Duignan & Duncan, 2003). The potential causal link between these factors appears to be an area needing further research.

Whilst this picture is derived from the perspective of aspiring leaders, the perspective of current principals is also worth noting. In 2002, a survey of 550 NSW DET primary principals revealed that these principals resented what they saw as a dysfunctional use of their time. Most principals stated clearly that their goal was to be motivational, visionary, pedagogical, educational and people-centred leaders within their school communities, not office-bound de-personalised site managers (Marks, 2002–03).

From competency to capability

More recent research among practising principals who are recognised by the employing authority (NSW DET) and their professional colleagues as being 'effective principals' has produced some important evidence about how they are analysing their own roles. When asked to identify the leadership capabilities of highest importance, these principals nominated, in order of importance: being able to remain calm under pressure; having a sense of humour; being able to keep work in perspective (work–life balance); having a clear, justified vision of where the school must head; being able to deal effectively with conflict situations; wanting to achieve the best outcomes possible for students; and being able to bounce back from adversity (Scott, 2003, p. 35).

A conclusion that can be drawn from the research of both Marks (2002–03) and Scott (2003) is that any future enhancement of the status, respect, efficiency and professionalism of the principalship will require a movement away from the dominance of a competencies-based orientation in their preparation and development programs towards a leadership capabilities philosophy and framework (Duignan, 2004a). I propose in the final chapter of this book that effective leadership development programs need to be redesigned to meet this need.

The distinction between 'competencies' and 'capabilities' in leadership training and development was made by Stephenson (1992 & 2000, p. 4). Capability, he stated (1992, p. 1), depends on our ability to use our knowledge and skills in complex and changing situations, rather than on simply possessing these skills, and capable people have confidence in their ability to 'take effective and appropriate action within unfamiliar and changing circumstances'. He defined the concept of capability as 'an all round human quality' involving the integration of knowledge, skills, personal qualities and understanding *used appropriately and effectively . . . in new and changing* circumstances' (Stephenson, 2000, p. 2, italics in original).

Competencies, Stephenson (1992) suggests are individual and measurable skills demonstrated and assessed against agreed standards of competency. They are useful for solving familiar problems in familiar contexts for which we have learned familiar solutions. Competencies involve the use of knowledge and skills within traditional, rational problem-solving approaches.

The challenges and problems reported by principals in many of the incidents described in earlier chapters in this book represent, however, uncertain and unpredictable circumstances that cannot usually be resolved by the application of a set of formulae or the use of learned competencies. Resolving complex problems requires leaders to draw from the heart and the spirit as well as the hands and the head. When facing complex situations involving competing or contested values or ethical principles, leaders need to draw on all their resources – knowledge, skills and wisdom – to exercise good judgement. Many of these are derived from the lessons of life's experiences; they are crafted from accumulated learning or earned, sometimes with great personal cost and sacrifice, from life's journey.

Capabilities, it would seem, are *not* a set of pre-packaged competencies to be used by a leader to solve specific problems in the workplace. Rather they denote a dynamic capacity to respond positively to changing circumstances. Capability involves making a difference, making people and conditions better. Such a developmental approach involves transforming the contexts in which we live as well as 'transforming lives, and transforming societies' (Eade, 1999, in Seddon, 2002, p. 24).

Leadership capability is not just having the potential to act but actually taking action to generate positive changes that improve people and contexts. Leadership capability constitutes social action at the organisational level aimed at building a group or organisation's capacity to learn and develop positively.

Commenting on the work of the economics Nobel Prize winner Amartya Sen, Seddon points out that 'expanding capabilities is seen as a way of enhancing development' and the challenge of development is to 'expand people's capabilities' so that they 'can lead the lives they value, and have reason to value, thereby removing "unfreedoms" that restrict people's preferred ways of living' (Sen, 1999, in Seddon, 2002, p. 100).

Seddon's perspective on capability powerfully informs our understanding of leadership as an empowering and capacity-building force for organisations, groups and individuals. He points out that to expand people's capabilities the contexts in which they live and work must be reshaped to empower people. This will change both the circumstances and content of their lives. In this sense, true leadership capability will require the creation of organisational contexts and environments that challenge and encourage those who work there to realise 'the various things a person may value doing or being' (Seddon, 2002, p. 100). Capability involves valuing both doing and being as a person and as a leader.

Leadership capability is, therefore, primarily concerned with expanding one's own and other people's capabilities so that all can lead valued and meaningful lives and, in so doing, making a significant difference in the lives of those they touch. In the case of school principals, it means that they need to be capable, relevant human beings who help create meaning in the lives of those who work and live with them. As capable leaders, principals need to have adequate knowledge, understanding and skills to discharge their responsibilities and resolve complex problems effectively. However, many of these 'skills of doing' can only be applied effectively if people also have the necessary 'skills of being'. Principals who have been exposed to development programs in, for example, interpersonal relations or conflict management, do not necessarily perform well in these areas. To 'do' good listening, a basic skill for both interpersonal relations and conflict management, requires the listener to 'be' patient, emotionally present, non-judgemental and sufficiently self-confident to avoid becoming defensive when hearing difficult things. No wonder that principals who have attended a short program in such areas often seem to lack the confidence, courage, commitment and wisdom to apply these skills in unfamiliar and changing circumstances.

Wisdom and capability

Principals, like any other people, may have many years' experience in leadership positions, but may not have distilled much wisdom from their experiences. Length of experience is no substitute for depth of experience – the 'inner wisdom' that leaders develop as they reflect on, critique, even agonise over, the meanings, implications and possible future applications of the lessons learned from their experiences. In this book, I am defining capable people as those who engage with the ethical and moral dimensions of life as well as the cognitive, factual and rational. They go beyond the competent person's rational analyses of facts and situations, and develop a 'wisdom way of knowing' that *engages their whole being* (Groome, 1998, italics added). That's the crucial difference: a wisdom way of knowing elevates mere facts, knowledge and competencies to the loftier heights of human endeavour, involving the whole person – head, hands, heart and spirit – in life-giving ways.

This connection between wisdom and capability in leaders and leadership is not often recognised in the literature, much less in the practice of leadership. Wisdom is often equated with 'intuition' or with having a 'gut feeling' about something or someone. In the argument presented here, 'gut feeling' encompasses the wisdom derived from experiences of life. It embraces the cognitive and practical as well as the emotive and spiritual dimensions of life, wrapping the cognitive and practical in wise emotive and spiritual frames to take a fully human view of situations. An important implication of this is that leaders need to develop their own capabilities and those of others so that their organisations can flourish in a complex, uncertain, unpredictable and rapidly changing environment. An underlying assumption of this argument is that development of personal and organisational capabilities, in an uncertain and complex organisational context, requires a leadership artistry that is unlikely to emerge from the acquisition of a generic set of management competencies through training or apprenticeship. Leaders who have to deal with unfamiliar problems in unfamiliar situations need to develop flexible mindsets and frameworks and to reach beyond the slavish application of predetermined practices and established procedures (Stephenson, 2000).

A capable leader is, first and foremost, a capable and confident human being. While knowledge and competencies are necessary ingredients, capable leaders also instil a deep sense of values and confidence in all those they touch through their leadership. Their sense of self-efficacy is contagious, thereby creating a learning culture in which all involved believe that they can be whatever they want to become.

A useful model to explain why contemporary leaders need to adopt new mindsets and modes of operation when confronted by 'unfamiliar problems' in 'unfamiliar contexts' (see Figure 8.1) is described by Stephenson (1992, p. 3 & 2000, p. 3). He concluded that in the past (and for some leaders still) the mode of operation for leaders was predominantly in Position Y in Figure 8.1. This is where leaders experience *familiar* problems within a *familiar* context. In Position Y, the concerns are for reliable delivery, performance standards, error elimination, technical expertise and the mastery of established procedures. The prevailing culture to support Position Y, according to Stephenson, is *training* and this approach, based on competencies, has dominated leadership and management development for a number of years.

However, Stephenson identifies Position Z (unfamiliar problems and unfamiliar context) as the contemporary reality for most leaders. In Position Z, even intelligent application of predetermined

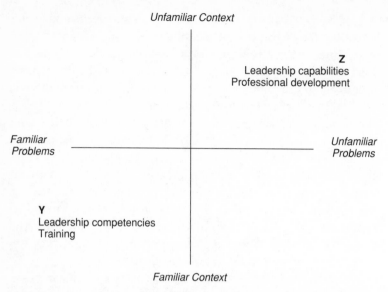

Figure 8.1 Stephenson (2000): *A Culture of 'Training' vs A Culture of 'Professional Development'*

practices can, he suggests, have disastrous results. This position involves a much greater use of what he calls 'leadership capabilities' which include: informal networks; creative problem solving; use of intuition; planned risk-taking; courage; imagination; reliance on beliefs and values; and highly developed self-awareness and self-knowledge. He argues that the culture to support Position Z is one of *professional development*. In the context of this argument, the concept of development, both personal and professional, is closely aligned to that of capability.

It seems clear, therefore, that leaders who have to make choices in complex and uncertain tension situations require more than management skills and competencies. They require creative, intuitive frameworks based on in-depth understanding of human nature and of the values, ethics, and moral dimensions inherent in human interaction and choice. They have to be emotionally mature enough to develop mutually elevating and productive relationships. Above all, they need wisdom derived from critical reflection on the meaning of life and work.

The ability of educational leaders to establish and nurture effective relationships within their organisations is essential if a shared leadership culture is to emerge and be sustained. Capable educational leaders, of course, will not try to run the show on their own. They will know that collaborating with key stakeholders is both necessary and desirable. I believe that it is time to take a fresh look at how leadership capacity is generated in many of our contemporary schools. Leadership, as both concept and practice, should be reinterpreted to include the contributions of all stakeholders. Leadership does not have to be the property of any one individual ('The Boss') or group ('Executive Team'); at its best, it grows out of the shared vision, beliefs and efforts of a committed group.

Of course, schools also require capable teachers. As with a capable leader, a capable teacher is, first and foremost, a capable and confident human being. Changes in curriculum, students' engagement, and teacher–student relationships must, of course, be made in order to improve student achievement, but these will not suffice. Above all, changes must occur in the hearts and minds of teachers (Townsend, 1998 & 1999). Capable teachers who move beyond competency towards greater flexibility and adaptability become truly professional. Helping to make teachers more capable (flexible, adaptable and professional) is a major contemporary and future challenge for educational leaders (Townsend, 1999, p. 34).

In the next chapter, I will argue that for educational leaders to respond capably to the challenges in chapter 2 and the tensions in chapter 3 they also need to become authentic educational leaders. As such, they promote and support authentic teaching and learning to optimise learning opportunities and outcomes for the students entrusted to their care.

Key ideas for reflection

Effective educational leaders have to be capable both as individuals and as professionals. They must be able to use their knowledge, skills and competencies confidently, with good judgement and wisdom, to solve complex problems in changing circumstances and contexts. The development of wisdom and good judgement cannot only be dependent upon competency-based training, which may well be inadequate as a basis for the leadership development and formation of capable educational leaders.

In this chapter it is recommended that educational leaders develop their leadership capabilities, as well as their knowledge base and competencies, in order to be capable leaders. By being capable, they will help bring about positive change; transform themselves, others and their school communities; and make a difference by strengthening the collective capacities of their school and school communities. Changes must also occur in the hearts and minds of teachers, in order for them to become more capable. Helping to make teachers more capable – more flexible, adaptable and professional – is a contemporary and future challenge for educational leaders.

Questions for reflection

- What do you understand to be the distinction between leadership competencies and leadership capabilities?
- What would be some key indicators of leadership capability in schools?
- In what ways can educational leaders develop their own leadership capabilities and those of others?
- What would be some of the key indicators of capable teachers?
- In what ways can educational leaders assist teachers to become more capable (flexible, adaptable and professional)?
- How can educational leaders help transform the collective capacity of their schools and communities to transform learners and learning?

Chapter 9

Why we need authentic educational leaders

Capable leaders are authentic leaders in terms of their values, intentions, practices and accomplishments. Authentic leaders engage in leadership actions and relationships that are ethical and moral (Terry, 1993). They are concerned with ethics and morality, especially as these relate to deciding what is significant, what is right and what is worthwhile (Duignan & Macpherson, 1992; Starratt, 1994; Sergiovanni, 1992). Such leadership elevates the actions of the leader above mere pragmatics or expediency (Hodgkinson, 1991); its focus is largely on 'elevating leaders' moral reasoning' (Terry, 1993, p. 46), which is central to Burns' (1978) seminal distinction between leadership that is transactional and that which is transformational. *Transactional* leaders are concerned with the everyday transactions that often consume a great deal of their time, but *transforming* leaders engage with others in ways that raise each other 'to higher levels of motivation and morality'; they are moral because they help raise 'the level of human conduct and ethical aspiration of both leader and led, and thus [they have] a transforming effect on both' (Burns, 1978, p. 20). So, in this book, what I mean by 'authentic leaders' are those capable, relevant human beings who transform the lives of those they touch; in the case of authentic educational leaders, those they touch most of all are their teaching colleagues, students, parents and their local school communities.

Authentic educational leadership

Authentic educational leaders help infuse educational practice with a higher purpose and meaning (Duignan & Bhindi, 1997;

Bhindi & Duignan, 1997). Such leadership should help *everybody* within a school community to be *somebody*, reducing feelings of anonymity and impotence and helping develop a sense of hope and of possibilities. In schools, authentic educational leaders, for example, pay close attention to the quality and impact of teaching and students' learning. They help create the conditions within which teachers and students take considerable responsibility for the quality of their own teaching and learning.

I am suggesting that while authentic leadership focuses on ethics and morality in actions and interactions, authentic *educational* leadership must also promote and support the core values of schooling. Authentic educational leaders challenge others to participate in the visionary activity of identifying in curriculum, in teaching and in learning what is worthwhile, what is worth doing and preferred ways of doing and acting together. They encourage both teachers and students to commit themselves to educational and professional practices that are, by their nature, educative (Duignan & MacPherson, 1992).

Authentic educational leaders are well aware that reflective teaching is the key to quality improvement in teaching and learning. They encourage teachers to reflect on the quality and effectiveness of their teaching and provide them with opportunities for such reflection (by allocating time in the timetable). They encourage teachers to strive for quality in their teaching, and support this through developing teams for innovative teaching approaches, and providing resources to enhance collaborative teaching and learning planning and practices. They promote, support and celebrate the efforts of those whose performance upholds the values of their school's culture, for example, reflective teaching and authentic learning processes.

Authentic educational leaders help promote the five NCSL pillars of distributed leadership discussed in chapter 7. These are: self-confident and self-effacing headship; clarity of structure and accountability; investment in leadership capability; a culture of trust; and a turning point – specific events that gave momentum to the distribution of leadership (NCSL, 2006, p. 22). They build leadership capacity through the promotion and support of shared and distributed leadership practices and they engage teachers in key decisions related to the promotion of authentic learning based on their knowledge of the contours of expertise in their schools, as discussed in chapter 7.

Authentic learning

Authentic teaching and learning, like authentic leadership, are moral activities because they engage both teachers and students in a deeper understanding of the nature and purpose of their lives and in determining how they can best contribute to the greater good of society. Authentic learning is not just about *taking* new knowledge and skills for oneself but is more about developing the capacity to give one's unique contribution to others. Authentic learning makes a difference in the lives of all those who engage in it.

The key characteristics of authentic learning are that students develop:
1 personal meaning from and through their learning;
2 awareness of the relationships between the self and the content of study;
3 respect for the integrity of the subject/object of study;
4 an appreciation of the implications of their learning for their lives outside the school;
5 an ability to apply their rich understanding of their learning in practice; and
6 their capabilities as authentic and capable human beings
   (Duignan & Bezzina, 2004 adapted from Starratt, 2004b).
While authentic educational leaders and most teachers want authentic learning opportunities and experiences for students in their schools, too frequently many students experience only 'inauthentic learning' (Starratt, 2004b). Inauthentic learning is characterised by: impersonal treatment of information by learners; a disconnect between the learner and the content being studied; thinking that learning equates to passing tests; regarding memorisation and regurgitation of facts as learning; and, most serious of all, students left fundamentally unchanged as human beings by their schooling experiences. By connecting learners' search for meaning

and purpose in their lives to a variety of personal meanings to be found in the academic curriculum, authentic educators enable their students as learners to continuously transform (construct, deconstruct, reconstruct) their understanding of themselves and 'place' themselves within the challenges and possibilities of their lives (Starratt, 2004a).

The concept of authentic learning has a close counterpoint in the idea of authentic pedagogy (Newman & Wehlage, 1995; Newman & Associates, 1996). Through intense dialogue between and amongst students and between students and their teachers, students are encouraged to generate new meanings and deeper understandings of complex issues related to the subject areas they are studying. Using a disciplined inquiry approach, teachers assist students to develop higher order thinking skills so as to intelligently interrogate questions of relevance to their learning and their lives outside the classrooms. In this way, students learn to value the integrity of the disciplines they are studying and attempt to make sense of them in terms of the challenges they are experiencing in their lives.

It would seem, therefore, that a central challenge for authentic educational leaders is to help bridge any gap that might exist between leadership and authentic learning and teaching. In a pilot project entitled 'Leaders transforming learners and learning' (LTLL Project, 2005–06), there is a planned and systematic attempt to transform both learners and learning in pilot schools by developing a close influencing connection between the leadership of these schools and their approaches to curriculum and pedagogy. LTLL draws on some key ideas of Starratt (2004a) to establish this connection.

Linking authentic leadership to authentic learning

As already discussed, the core focus for authentic educational leaders needs to be on the enhancement of authentic teaching and learning. This focus challenges them to be more fully present to the transformative possibilities of students' learning and to be more proactively responsible for inviting teachers to create learning opportunities and experiences for their students that will help transform their lives.

That is why the corporate–managerialist approaches to educational leadership cannot succeed. The distinction between educational leaders and business leaders was highlighted by Gross and Shapiro (2005, p. 2) when they argued that educators and educational leaders 'have a very different set of values from those who focus on corporate life'. Educational leaders are accountable, not to shareholders, but to stakeholders who are, essentially, students, their families and their communities. The aim is not for short-term profits but for the generation of an ethical and just society. '*While business is transactional, our work is transformational*' (p. 2, italics in original).

The work of authentic educational leaders is transformational insofar as they promote and support transformational teaching and learning for their students. To do this they must bring their deepest principles, beliefs, values and convictions to their work. The ethic of authenticity is at the very heart and soul of educational leadership as it points the way towards a more self-responsible form of relationships and leadership (Starratt, 2004a). Authentic educational leaders act with the good of others (e.g. students, teachers, parents) as a primary reference. Authenticity involves educational leaders in reciprocal relationships and 'the authentic educator is involved in authentic relationships with learners' (Starratt, 2004a, p. 81).

It is this engagement of the 'self' with the 'other' that provides the authentic educator and the authentic educational leader with a deep sense of responsibility for what is happening to the other. In the school setting, this 'ethic of responsibility' is focused primarily on the core people – teachers and students – and the core business – authentic teaching and learning (Starratt, 2004a).

Authentic educational leaders feel deeply responsible for the authenticity of the learning of students in their schools. They name, challenge and change, if at all possible, teaching practices that promote inauthentic learning (e.g. teaching narrowly to focus on tests). They have the courage of their convictions and stand up for what they see as ethically and morally 'right', especially with regard to the ways in which teachers and students engage with learning content and processes.

Of course authentic educational leaders, including teachers as leaders of learning, need to be aware of the type and quality of teaching and learning that is occurring in their schools and classrooms. They should engage in personal reflection and whole-school dialogue on the degree to which the conditions necessary for authentic learning are present. A short reflective instrument or tool is included as Figure 9.1 to encourage educational leaders and teachers to focus on some key evidence of the existence or otherwise of these conditions.

Analysing your leadership authenticity

The purpose of this short instrument is to help you reflect on your own authenticity as an educational leader and on how evident the conditions for authentic learning are in your school. The instrument is a tool to provide information about current conditions for authenticity and authentic learning in your school and to encourage reflection on them as a basis for action and professional formation.

The scores are meant only as indications of strengths and areas needing attention. The idea is to generate discussion among staff so as to sustain and build on the strengths and develop strategies to bring about improvement in the areas requiring attention. You are encouraged to add other items to the instrument that are relevant to your self, school and situation (see Figure 9.1).

The answers to the items on the instrument can help educational leaders decide how to influence the shape and direction of the learning environment better. Influence is normally most effective if educational leaders demonstrate their presence to others through their relationships. The concept of 'presence' is receiving increasing attention in educational leadership in terms of its importance in developing meaningful relationships.

Authentic educational leaders are 'present' to and for others

Authentic educational leaders are 'present' to teachers, students and their parents and to the conditions of learning in their schools. Presence, according to Starratt (2004a), can be regarded as an ethic underpinning authentic educational leadership. It means being there, in numerous ways, for others. It implies attention and sensitivity to others and each other and the development of personal and professional relationships so that 'our presence activates our authenticity and the authenticity of others' (Starratt, 2004a, p. 91).

Leadership authenticity
(Adapted from LTLL Project, 2005–06)

Authenticity demands that we act in truth and integrity in all our actions and interactions as humans, educators and educational leaders.

Indicator As a leader I:	Evidence (What are the visible signs that this indicator is present in my school?)	Rating 1 – Not at all evident to 4 – Strongly evident 1 2 3 4			
1 reflect and act upon my values and ethical standards					
2 encourage others to reflect upon and discover their own authenticity					
3 encourage and support authenticity in mutually rewarding relationships					
4 engage with others in such ways that all are raised to higher levels of motivation and morality					
5 work hard to create authentic conditions in the workplace					
6 demonstrate passion and commitment to the promotion and support of authentic teaching and learning					
7 help transform learning and learners so that they can lead more responsible, productive, meaningful and fulfilling lives					
8 seek to make a positive difference in the lives of all those I (we) touch					
Total of ratings					
*Mean score for authenticity (Total / Number of items)					

* A total score of 16 or below, or a mean score of 2 or below, would indicate a need to pay closer attention to developing your leadership authenticity and that of the school's culture. Examining each item's score will indicate which areas are strong and which need improvement.

Figure 9.1 Instrument for reflecting on leadership authenticity

In a number of the cases discussed in chapter 3, the principals involved were both personally and professionally present to and for those who were affected by the conditions of the case. The principal in the case of the girl whose grandfather took her to live with an aunt was sensitive to the circumstances of the girl (whose mother, a single parent, was on drugs and not able to care properly for her child at the time) and managed the situation in a way that focused on the girl's needs. Similarly, the principal in the case of the disadvantaged boy who received the blue slip for discipline problems just before the athletics carnival was present for that child and supported his inclusion in the event. The principal in the case of the elderly teacher with beginning dementia was greatly concerned for her welfare and was present for her and her husband as well as the students at the school. Being present in cases like these means that the principal is fully aware of the details of the situation and is sufficiently concerned and motivated to take action to help rectify the situation.

Presence represents 'both a state of mind and a way of behaving' in relationships (Halpern & Lubar, 2003, p. 9). These authors have developed a model of presence in leadership which they base on their experiences as actors on the stage. Good actors, they point out, are 'fully present in the moment' which means that they engage totally, without distraction, with their role. Being present, they say, is the first requirement of acting – 'be there, in the moment, alive, energized' (p. 19). With regard to leadership, they recommend that influential leaders are fully present in their world; they are 'totally in the moment, undistracted by anything past or future, sharp as a razor, alive to everything around you' (p. 25). They claim that as a leader 'you're at your best when you're totally in the moment, totally focused'.

Their model of leadership presence, which they refer to as the PRES model, consists of four closely aligned, sequential yet integrated, elements. These are:

- **P** stands for *Being Present*, the ability to be completely in the moment, and flexible enough to handle the unexpected;
- **R** stands for *Reaching Out*, the ability to build relationships with others through empathy, listening, and authentic connection;

- **E** stands for *Expressiveness*, the ability to express feelings and emotions appropriately by using all available means – words, voice, body, face – to deliver one congruent message; and
- **S** stands for *Self-knowing*, the ability to accept yourself, to be authentic, and to reflect your values in your decisions and actions (Halpern & Lubar, 2003, p. 9, italics in the original).

Each element 'builds on, and gains power from, the preceding element' (Halpern & Lubar, 2003, p. 10). However, they pointed out that to be self-knowing about where you came from and what you stand for is 'to be authentic', and it helps integrate all the elements of the PRES model in everyday actions and interactions.

This idea of leadership presence – emphasising being fully present in the moment to and for others; building relationships based on authentic connections; expressing oneself with feeling and emotion; and knowing and accepting self – is compatible with the characteristics of authentic educational leadership already discussed. Without presence it is difficult to see how effective relationships can occur, and without effective relationships educational leaders have little influence.

While Halpern and Lubar emphasise the importance of being present in the moment, Senge *et al.* (2004, p. 11) incorporate an important future perspective into the meaning of presence. After all, educational leadership is usually future-driven, as it is primarily concerned with teachers' and students' growth and improvement. Senge *et al.* regard presence as an active process that is guided by, and no doubt guides, the choices we make for the future. They suggest that 'the core capacity needed for accessing the field of the future is presence'. While presence can mean being present in the moment, it also has an element of letting go of old, no longer useful ideas and 'letting come' new ideas and perspectives. In this way 'the forces shaping a situation can shift from re-creating the past to manifesting or realizing an emerging future' (p. 11).

This evolutionary and futuristic perspective on the concept of leadership presence is most illuminating about what educational leaders need to do to bring about transformation in learners, learning and teaching in schools. Authentic educational leaders need to ask themselves how their leadership can move beyond continuously re-creating the past to continuously constructing an emerging future. They need to ask what 'being fully present' means in relation to their leadership of the school, including the teaching and learning of students in their schools, but it also means naming and challenging 'inauthentic teaching and learning' and taking positive action to bring about change and 'letting come' new and creative ways of teaching to support authentic learning.

Authentic learning, for Halpern and Lubar (2003), is '. . . a never-ending journey of personal experience' (p. 232). They point out that learning from personal experience, especially about yourself, can lead to personal transformation, thereby becoming a new person – a new you. To learn is not to *have* but to *be* (p. 234, italics added). What more can authentic educational leaders hope for with regard to the children under their care?

Leadership presence demands personal formation and growth and makes taking responsibility for nurturing the growth and development of others natural. Leadership presence is about taking responsibility for what is happening in your sphere of influence. Authentic educational leaders couldn't 'live with themselves' (ethic of authenticity) unless they took responsibility for the quality of students' learning (ethic of responsibility) by naming and challenging inauthentic teaching and learning and then helping create the conditions to transform them (ethic of presence). Their presence activates a deep sense of their own authenticity and that of others. Injustice offends their sense of authenticity and generates a response that is consistent with 'the person I am, the values I embrace, and my commitment to others as a human being' (Starratt, 2004a, p. 77).

Authentic educational leaders who are fully present develop the '. . . capacity to avoid imposing old frameworks on new realities' (Senge *et al.* 2004, p. 84) and therefore encourage and support creative thinking, while challenging many contemporary teaching and learning paradigms and practices. This may be challenging for many of the educational systems in which they work.

Many educational leaders, however, should develop a greater sense of their presence for others, especially for those who are vulnerable or in need. As suggested earlier concerning their leadership authenticity, they should engage in personal reflection on, and analysis of, the degree to which they are present to and for others within their school and school community. A short reflective instrument or tool is included as Figure 9.2 to encourage a focus on some key evidence of their presence or lack of it in their school.

Analysing your leadership presence

As with the instrument on leadership authenticity, this instrument is meant to generate discussion and dialogue with a view to bringing about improvement. The scores suggest trends only. You may wish to add additional items to this instrument that are relevant to your self, school or situation (see Figure 9.2).

To be fully present to others is a great challenge for many educational leaders. They are frequently distracted by the hectic pace of life and work, and eschew opportunities for reflection on their practice and the deep learning required to bring about transformation in self and others. They may find it difficult to engage more fully (to be fully present) with those with whom they work because they lack the emotional intelligence to be open, trusting, and authentically reciprocal in their relationships. Those driven by corporate, bureaucratic and hierarchical imperatives may devalue the integrity of others by lacking respect for them as capable human beings. The pressures of intense individualism may very well have robbed them of the generosity of spirit that is a hallmark of authentic educational leaders.

In case you think I am being too harsh in my criticism, I want to say that I do not necessarily place the blame for this state of affairs entirely on the shoulders of educational leaders themselves. They live in a world of uncertainty and rapid change that constantly challenges extant paradigms. One need only examine the major changes in the context of schooling in recent years to appreciate the enormity of the challenges facing teachers and educational leaders in schools. Schools must now keep up with changes in technology, with new generations of hardware and software exploding onto the market every few months. Educated and discerning students and parents challenge the way things are done in schools at increasing rates. Legal imperatives, government and public accountability pressures and processes are ever more complex and demanding. Schools are no longer protected fiefdoms where

Leadership presence
(Adapted from LTLL Project, 2005–06)

The concept of presence challenges us to engage purposefully and meaningfully with others in ways that are authentic and morally uplifting.

Indicator As a leader I:	Evidence (What are the visible signs that this indicator is present in my school?)	Rating 1 – Not at all evident to 4 – Strongly evident 1	2	3	4
1 value the importance of full awareness of self in relation to others					
2 create opportunities for self reflection/critique					
3 value and act upon presence to/for the other that is affirming					
4 value and act upon presence that is sensitive to others					
5 value and act upon presence to/for others that is enabling and encouraging of their capacity for meaningful participation in the life of the school					
6 identify and change the obstacles to my presence to/for others					
7 value and act upon presence to students so as to create conditions for their growth and transformation					
8 commit to formation and development that enhances my presence to/for others					
Total of ratings					
*MEAN SCORE FOR PRESENCE (Total /Number of items)					

* A total score of 16 or below, or a mean score of 2 or below, would indicate a need to pay closer attention to developing/increasing your leadership presence. Examining each item's score will indicate which areas are strong and which need improvement with regard to your leadership presence.

Figure 9.2 Instrument for reflecting on leadership presence

teachers and leaders can do their own things, in their own way, in their own time.

In my nearly four decades as an educator, I have witnessed a transformation in the context and conditions of education and schooling. My six-year-old grandson, Matthew, uses a laptop computer while I used an abacus (we called it a 'ballframe') at his age. How well are teachers and other educational leaders in schools prepared for this brave new world? Have leadership preparation and development programs kept up with this rapid pace of change? Are educational leaders trying to impose, as Senge put it, 'old frameworks on new realities'?

How well have teachers and educational leaders been supported in their professional development by the systems for which they work? As discussed in chapter 8, many school principals believe that their experiences with competency-based professional development programs have not prepared them well for the challenges they currently face (Marks, 2002–03).

I propose that educational leaders, including teachers, need more than competency-based training and development, they need *formation*, not only in terms of the development of ethical and moral frameworks for action, but also in forming them as capable, authentic human beings. They require opportunities to develop unique capabilities that combine intellectual and moral dimensions, to succeed in a world that is frequently driven by the economic and materialistic forces and relativistic values discussed in chapter 1, as well as rapid technological and social change. We cannot assume, for example, that if we equip educational leaders with knowledge and competencies related to collaboration and sharing that it will actually happen in the workplace. Sharing requires the capacity to be fully present, and presence can only be achieved and maintained by capable and authentic human beings.

They also need opportunities, in their formation as leaders, to engage with ethical and moral frameworks that have both theoretical (nature of ethics and ethical perspectives) and practical (living ethics) dimensions. Recent scandals in business and service organisations clearly signal the need for such formation.

In the next chapter, I want to explore further the idea of educational leaders as capable and authentic human beings, as well as the need to move to leadership capabilities as a basis for their formation.

Key ideas for reflection

Authentic educational leaders challenge others to participate in the visionary activity of identifying in curriculum, teaching and learning what is worthwhile, what is worth doing and preferred ways of doing and acting together. They encourage both teachers and students to commit themselves to educational and professional practices that are intensely educative.

They also help create the conditions in which teachers and students take considerable responsibility for the quality of their own teaching and learning. They engage especially with teachers, students and parents in ways that raise everybody to higher levels of motivation and morality.

A major challenge for educational leaders is to help transform many contemporary educational contexts and processes characterised by traditional (some would argue inauthentic) approaches to teaching and learning and create, instead, the conditions within which authentic leadership, teaching and learning can grow and flourish. While leaders need to focus on developing authenticity and presence because these can lead to personal, ethical and professional formation and growth, they can also involve teachers in taking responsibility for and nurturing the growth and development of students. Leadership presence involves knowing about and taking responsibility for what is happening in your sphere of influence.

Questions for reflection

Leadership authenticity

- What values guide my life and work?
- What have been some of my character-forming experiences (both positive and negative)?
- How do I make a difference in the lives of others?
- What values and qualities define my relationships and my leadership?

- What gives me strength to deal with difficult situations involving 'people challenges' and difficult ethical tensions?
- How well do I reconcile (balance) my 'self' with my current work 'role'?

Leadership presence

- In what ways are you 'present' to/for your professional colleagues?
- In what ways are you present to/for your students?
- Who is fully present to/for you? How does he/she do this?
- How could you be more fully present to the challenges inherent in authentic/inauthentic learning?
- How can you, as a leader, be more fully present to the people you work with and the conditions of their work?

Chapter 10

Forming capable and authentic educational leaders

Given the nature of the challenges and tensions discussed in chapters 2 and 3, principals and other educational leaders in schools will, I believe, need to be supported and developed in special ways. The short cases presented in chapter 3 represent many of the daily challenges and tensions faced by educational leaders in schools. As was discussed earlier, resolving such tensions calls upon more than an educational leader's knowledge and skills; it requires the application of good judgement, intuition and wisdom, as well as logic and reason. As was evident from the conclusions in Marks' (2002–03) research reported in chapter 8, many contemporary competency-driven leadership development programs do not prepare educational leaders for decision-making involving contestation of values and ethical tensions.

In chapters 7, 8 and 9, I suggested that educational leaders need to have the capacity to share their leadership responsibilities with other key stakeholders in their school communities; develop their leadership capabilities both as individuals and as professionals; and practice authentic leadership, especially by being present to and for others in their school community. Educational leadership development programs (e.g. short courses and mentoring), as currently constituted, indicate a genuine commitment to the continuous improvement of leadership practice in schools, but if we wish to create organisations that are alive with shared and distributed leadership and leaders who are capable of leading in tension-filled, ethically-charged situations, a more holistic perspective of what constitutes leadership preparation and development needs to be generated and implemented.

The starting point, I suggest, for the development of capable, authentic educational leaders is personal formation and transformation, leading to a deep understanding of their personal values and a passionate conviction that they can, through shared leadership approaches, make a difference in the lives of their colleagues and the students in their care.

A formation approach to leadership development is essentially an educative process which involves '. . . a pursuit of the verities (truth, beauty, goodness, justice, happiness, self-fulfilment)' (Hodgkinson, 1991, p. 17). In the midst of the current instrumental, utilitarian, economically rationalist view of education and educational leadership discussed in chapter 1, Hodgkinson's words urge all educators and educational leaders to form and transform themselves personally and professionally. To help leaders do this, we may need to rethink much of what currently passes for educational leadership development.

Why we need formation programs

Education is 'the art of calling others to seek the truth as to what it means to be human' (Hodgkinson, 1991, p. 17). 'What it means to be human' is the key to understanding and forming educational leaders as capable and authentic human beings and leaders. Formational experience should be uplifting, humanising and transformational. While an economic rationalist approach to education may ensure our survival as a species, educating, as a moral and transforming force, will ensure that the human struggle for survival is worthwhile, as it helps us generate purpose and meaning to our existence (Hodgkinson, 1991).

I was intrigued recently to notice a chapter entitled 'Leadership: Becoming a human being' in Senge *et al.*'s 2004 book *Presence: Human purpose and the field of the future*. In it, Senge suggested that one of the oldest ideas about leadership is that 'with power must come wisdom', but that most organisations' commitment to 'cultivate moral development has all but vanished' (pp. 183–184). He defined cultivation as involving 'a capacity for delayed gratification, for seeing longer term effects of actions, for achieving quietness of mind', which both the ancient Greeks and the Chinese believed 'required a lifetime of dedicated personal work, guided by masters' (p. 184).

In the same chapter, one of Senge's co-authors, Flowers, suggested that some people believe that these old ideas don't speak to the realities of today's technology-driven world, and too many of our leaders are 'more likely to be technologists than philosophers', focused more on obtaining and using power, and 'maintaining an appearance of control' (p. 184).

In attempting to chart a new path for leadership, Senge *et al.* (2004, p. 215) suggested that there are two basic options if we wish to 'reverse the growing gap between our power and our wisdom': first 'to limit the expansion of technology' (an unlikely one); and second 'to find ways that lead to increasing reliance on enhancing human development and wisdom'.

The latter option is a very significant statement and reinforced for me many of the leadership formational ideas presented in this chapter. Enhancing human development and wisdom might seem like a tall order and an unrealistic expectation for a leadership formation program, but it puts the emphasis in the right place – the heart and soul, as well as the head and hands, of leaders.

This is not to say that formation approaches should neglect knowledge acquisition and cognitive development (Duignan 2002a & 2005). A formation program for leaders should be intellectually challenging, and complement other educational experiences in the cultivation of the intellect. Knowledge acquisition, however, is not an end in itself. Although leaders require knowledge that is professionally useful, it is the skills involved in the generation, critique and synthesis of knowledge that are essential for leaders '. . . to fill their respective posts in life better, and of making them more intelligent, capable, active members of society' (Newman, 1915, p. xxxvi). Formation processes and experiences should assist leaders to develop their ethical and moral frameworks for the study and analysis of the complex problems and tensions they face every day. Their challenge is to combine the intellectual and the moral into frameworks that transcend knowledge generation and skill development, and rise to the challenge of reflective critique of contemporary dilemmas and tensions, and nurturing their personal and professional formation through a deeper exploration of what it means to be a capable human being in the twenty-first century.

In a recent reading of Newman's (1915) classic treatise *On the scope and nature of university education*, I was struck by its contemporary relevance and practical implications. He argued that while the acquisition of knowledge could be regarded as an end in itself, its pursuit is a work of discipline and habit that helps develop a cultivated intellect for life. Newman (writing in the gendered style of his day) argued that in the absence of a cultivated mind, a person:

> . . . may not realise what his mouth utters; he may not see with his mental eye what confronts him; he may have no grasp of things as they are; or at least he may have no power at all of advancing one step forward of himself, in consequence of what he has already acquired, no power of discriminating between truth and falsehood; of sifting out the grains of truth from the mass, of arranging things according to their real value, and, if I may use the phrase, of building up ideas . . . The bodily eye, the organ for apprehending material objects, is provided by nature; the eye of the mind, of which the object is truth, is the work of discipline and habit (Newman, 1915, p. 145).

In attempting to develop a rationale and justification for providing educational leaders with formation programs that are intellectually challenging and rigorous, I discovered how relevant Newman's chapter 'Liberal knowledge viewed in relation to professionals' is for today's world. He stated (p. 172) that a cultivated intellect is 'emphatically *useful*' as it enables the professional:

> . . . to fill any post with credit, and to master any subject with facility. It shows him how to accommodate himself to others, how to throw himself into their state of mind, how to bring before them his own, how to influence them, how to come to an understanding with them, how to bear with them; . . . he knows when to speak and when to be silent; he is able to converse; he is able to listen; he can ask a question pertinently, and gain a lesson seasonably, when he

has nothing to impart himself; he is ever ready, yet never in the way; he is a pleasant companion, and a comrade you can depend upon; he knows when to be serious and when to trifle, and he has a sure tact which enables him to trifle with gracefulness and to be serious with effect.

Surely, these characteristics are those of the capable authentic educational leader which we have discussed, at length, in the previous chapter. They also appear to me to be relevant to what Senge *et al.* (2004) meant when they talked about enhancing human development and wisdom. Leader formation programs should be carefully constructed to ensure that they assist participants to further develop and refine the culture of their intellects. Such programs should adopt an interdisciplinary approach to expand participants' horizons and to enable them to better appreciate that intelligence is holistic, connecting them to the universe of knowledge and to their wholeness as human beings.

Leadership formation programs should also recognise the realities with which educational leaders deal on a daily basis and should ensure that assumptions are challenged and existing paradigms critiqued in relation to ethical and moral standards and contemporary knowledge and understandings. Such formation programs should prepare educational leaders for the future, not the past.

In this regard, Hesburgh (1994, p. 9), commenting on the contribution of Notre Dame University in contemporary society, suggested that: 'We cannot be satisfied here with medieval answers to modern questions'. He argued the need to combine the intellectual and the moral into a framework that transcends knowledge generation and critique, instead focusing on the development of the goodness and beauty of the human person. He stated that:

> . . . we are united in believing that intellectual virtues and moral values are important to life and to this institution [Notre Dame University], and we are totally committed to the development of wisdom, which is something more than knowledge and much akin to goodness and beauty when it radiates throughout a human person (Hesburgh, 1994, p. 8).

Formation, however, does not mean being shaped by a narrow ideology. It involves both a letting go of outmoded thinking and practices and a 'letting come' (Senge *et al.* 2004) of new, more appropriate, and useful ones. It constitutes opening our eyes, hearts and minds to new possibilities. O'Donohue (1997, pp. 89–92) likens this letting go and letting come to awaking from our slumber or our comfort zone and choosing with which eye we wish to see. He recommends that we should try to see with the loving eye where everything is possible. It is this loving eye that helps us to challenge our fixed paradigms and mindsets and makes us alert to the opportunities and possibilities of an emerging future so that we do not merely recreate the past. O'Donohue suggests that the loving eye helps you rise above '. . . the pathetic arithmetic of blame and judgement . . .' (p. 92) and it:

> . . . sees through and beyond image and affects the deepest change. Vision is central to your presence and creativity. To recognise *how* you see things can bring you self-knowledge and enable you to glimpse the treasures your life secretly holds. (pp. 92–93)

Formation programs for educational leaders should help them open their eyes to the possibilities in themselves and in others, and to the development of their capability to frame new paradigms of leadership, based on new orientations to relationships and presence, in order to respond effectively to the challenges and tensions discussed in chapters 2 and 3.

In these challenging times, educational leaders need to be open to new ways of thinking and doing, so as to maximise their influence on curriculum, pedagogy, teaching and learning. Leadership is usually defined as an influencing process, and authentic educational leaders have the awesome responsibility of influencing the young people in their care to become significant and worthwhile human beings. When addressing principals in New Zealand, Cardinal Williams (2000) reminded them of this challenge:

> To you Principals I want to say that, if ever you become discouraged, then know that part of you will be flying with every pilot, building with every architect, diagnosing with every doctor, creating with

every artist, fashioning with every craftsman and woman. More than that, part of you will be woven into the fabric of every sound marriage and every good home. You are making your way into the hearts and minds of the children and youth you teach (pp. 2–3).

If ever we needed reminding of the importance of the formation of educational leaders, including teachers, these words surely cut to the heart of the matter. Authentic educational leaders are in no small way responsible for ensuring that conditions are created in their schools and school communities that challenge students and teachers to explore the essence of their being and to seek the truth about what it means to be human. To meet this challenge, they need a type of formation that is not normally provided by typical educational leadership training and development programs, especially the competency-based training currently in vogue in many educational jurisdictions.

Leadership capabilities

The distinction between leadership competencies and leadership capabilities was discussed in chapter 8. It suggested that the intent of leadership formation programs should be to form educational leaders who are capable and authentic; who take action to bring about transformational change; who raise themselves and others to higher levels of motivation and morality; and who infuse their leadership practices with higher purpose and meaning. Their language of authenticity should not be empty jargon or an empty ideology. I believe that formation programs for educational leaders will be judged to be successful if they assist educational systems and schools to develop the capabilities of their leaders so that they make a difference in their sphere of influence in education and in life. The tensions inherent in the leadership challenges identified in the research study that supports many of the ideas in this book call for educational leaders to develop creative frameworks for choice and action that transcend knowledge acquisition, competencies and management skills. They need to develop their capabilities as capable, authentic human beings and leaders, as discussed in chapters 8 and 9.

Authentic educational leaders require a number of leadership capabilities to deal with the tension-filled environment of contemporary schools. These are described in this chapter and build on the work of Duignan and Burford (2002), Duignan *et al.* (2003), Spry and Duignan (2003), and Spry (2004). These capabilities are not necessarily discrete entities, but taken together form a framework for leaders who are faced with making challenging decisions in situations of complexity, uncertainty, unpredictability and ambiguity. They can also be used as a framework to develop the type of leadership formation programs discussed later.

The formation and/or further development of these capabilities cannot be achieved through traditional competency-based professional development programs or experiences. Such programs focus, almost exclusively, on imparting physical (including technical), social and mental skills. They tend to neglect the intellectual discipline, moral fortitude, wisdom and good judgement required for these skills to be transformed into leadership capabilities that prepare educational leaders to make wise and informed decisions in conditions of uncertainty and constant change.

The capabilities can be categorised into personal, relational, professional, and organisational (based on work by Spry & Duignan, 2003; Spry, 2004; Duignan, 2005; LTLL Project, 2005–06). There is obvious overlap among a number of the capabilities in the different categories but this is not a concern as the capabilities and their categories are meant only to provide a framework for formation activities and programs for educational leaders. I recommend that those responsible for the development and delivery of leadership development programs closely examine these capabilities. While the list is a long one, it is not meant to be exhaustive or exclusive. Those developing and implementing leadership formation programs could use them as an indicative list, expanding and modifying the language as necessary to better suit particular contexts and needs and selecting those capabilities that are relevant to leaders in their particular roles and contexts. They can also add others they believe to be absent from this list that are relevant to their roles and context.

It is unlikely that one person, for example the principal, is capable in all these areas. This is why shared and distributed leadership are such important models. These capabilities will be required by the collective leadership of the school, if they are to meet the expectations for and requirements of leadership in twenty-first century schools as well as to respond effectively to the challenges and tensions discussed in chapters 2 and 3.

A capability means more than simply possessing particular knowledge and skills or having the potential to do something. It means demonstrating that one can actually do it.

Personal capabilities

- **Is self-reflective** – Exhibits habits of critiquing personal motivations, beliefs, values and behaviours; takes personal strengths and limitations into account in decision-making; and commits to personal growth and improvement.
- **Demonstrates intellectual acuity** – Leadership demands a high level of mental acuity and discernment; effective educational leaders need disciplined minds and must be knowledgeable and rigorous in their methods of analysis and reasoning.
- **Displays a sense of self-efficacy and personal identity** – Projects a strong sense of self; and acts from a clear set of values and high ethical standards.
- **Uses intuition as well as logic and reason** – Shows, especially in decision-making, that intuition and wisdom are as important as logic and reason.
- **Projects confidence, optimism and resilience** – Believes and acts from a clear vision; maintains a positive outlook and views challenges as opportunities; shows a sense of curiosity and enthusiasm; gets going when the going is tough; and bounces back from adversity.
- **Exemplifies honesty and integrity** – Applies ethical standards to complex and perplexing tension situations; is impelled by core values and lives by those values; accepts the personal consequences of difficult choices and decisions; respects the integrity of others; and is open and honest in all dealings.
- **Demonstrates ethically responsible behaviours** – Acts as a thoughtful, caring human being, and not as a self-serving narcissist; lives by high ethical standards.

- **Is morally courageous** – Demonstrates strength of character and stands up for his/her values even against the expectations, wishes or demands of a popular majority.
- **Is spiritually connected** – Creates an environment rich in spiritual chemistry, based on a deep respect for the dignity and worth of everyone in the organisation and on a sense that there is something purposeful about life and relationships (interconnectedness) that transcends the narrow boundaries of the self and gives special meaning to one's existence. Also exhibits generosity of heart and spirit in relationships with fellow humans.
- **Displays imagination and vision** – Imagines what the future could be; articulates a personal sense of purpose and direction; and communicates this vision with purpose and influence.
- **Integrates work and personal life** – Balances the demands of family, community and personal life with work; maintains good health in terms of physical and mental wellbeing; and derives meaning and energy from a balanced and integrated life.

Relational capabilities

- **Is relationally adept** – Develops positive and productive relationships, especially with work colleagues; nurtures strong interpersonal skills, as well as mutually respectful and rewarding relationships.
- **Is emotionally mature** – Engages with others in mature, interdependent and mutually beneficial relationships; shows sensitivity to the emotions displayed by individuals and groups in given situations and uses emotions appropriately in relationships and decision-making.
- **Communicates with influence** – Displays open, informed and meaningful communication with others; engages purposefully with others and gains commitment from them through constructive dialogue on important challenges and problems; actively listens and allows time for others.
- **Is authentically present** – Demonstrates a genuine interest in and concern for people; acts with the good of others, especially those who are vulnerable or in need of assistance, as a primary reference; engages fully with others and is attentive and sensitive to the signals they send out.

- **Displays a trusting disposition** – Accepts a positive human anthropology; seeks out others and values their opinions and ideas; builds an inclusive community by seeking to forge personal and professional bonds with others.
- **Cultivates collaborative working environments** – Engages others in mutually beneficial relationships; uses resources to support collaboration; keeps vision, goals and purpose to the fore in all working relationships.
- **Engages in positive politics** – Identifies the key people or groups affected by a problem or decision; understands the interest of key stakeholders and their power; builds positive relationships, coalitions and alliances; learns from 'the opposition'; deals openly with difference and negotiates win-win (right-right) solutions.
- **Nurtures leadership capability in others** – Shares and distributes leadership responsibilities; creates an environment where risk-taking is supported and learning from mistakes is encouraged; encourages, nurtures and supports others to engage in leadership activities.

Professional capabilities

- **Is contextually aware and responsive** – Shows appreciation for the wider context of education and of significant emerging challenges; demonstrates leadership in a rapidly changing environment; seeks and implements new ideas and approaches to meet the challenges of change; helps shape a future of hope.
- **Inspires a collegial purpose and vision** – Articulates a vision and invites others to participate in communicating and implementing the vision; seeks to embody this vision in the goals, policies, programs, structures and operations of the organisation; celebrates the vision in the day-to-day activities of the school; encourages and supports professional teams and teamwork.
- **Displays curriculum and pedagogical know-how** – Is aware of theoretical developments in teaching and learning; nurtures effective learning environments for a wide range of students; supports school-based curriculum development; monitors and supports curriculum innovation.

- **Focuses on educational outcomes and accountability** – Delivers on intended outcomes; monitors and evaluates teaching and learning with appropriate evaluative tools; uses appropriate feedback processes and evaluation results to improve teaching and learning; and keeps stakeholders informed of progress.
- **Engages in and supports professional learning** – Shows commitment to continuous growth and learning; plans professional learning opportunities for self and others; connects professional learning to the core activities of learning and teaching.
- **Demonstrates professional commitment** – Serves others (e.g. students, teachers, parents, community) with passion and expertise; discharges professional duties responsibly and with care; adopts a life-long commitment to personal and professional formation and development; lives by professional codes of conduct and acts in ways that enhance the image of their profession.

Organisational capabilities

- **Engages in strategic thinking** – Demonstrates an awareness of the big picture; responds to all challenges with determination, confidence and foresight; avoids imposing old paradigms on new realities or constantly re-creating the past; constantly challenges key stakeholders to envision a dynamic future; involves others in contributing to the process of shaping strategic direction on an on-going basis; builds on current strengths to create a desired future.
- **Develops organisational capacity to respond to contemporary and future expectations of key stakeholders** – Continuously scans the environment and develops strategic readiness for most expectations and eventualities; builds organisational capacity to respond to contemporary and future expectations of key stakeholders; gives high priority to creating organisational structures and processes that are adaptable and flexible enough to respond to rapid and continuous change; demonstrates the capacity to lead positive change.
- **Builds a sharing organisational culture that focuses energies and talents on achieving high quality outcomes** – Helps

create the conditions for collaborative teaching and learning; maximises engagement with and involvement of teachers and students in planning and delivering quality learning experiences; encourages and supports authentic teaching and learning; implements processes to generate evidence-based outcomes.

- **Constructs creative designs for the use of people, time, space and technologies** – Critiques current use of these key resources and adjusts the balance to maximise learning and teaching effects; matches quantity and combination of these resources to the specific needs and mix of students and the specific learning environment; is technologically competent.
- **Models cultural sensitivity** – Shows sensitive discernment with regard to human and cultural differences, and consideration and empathy for those who may not share their perspectives or preferences.
- **Demonstrates managerial aptitude** – Possesses and uses the knowledge and competencies to manage people and resources in constructive and inspirational ways so as to achieve the purposes, goals and priorities of the organisation. Specifically, engages in creative job design and formative performance management; prepares budgets for areas of responsibility and employs responsible accounting procedures; builds organisational knowledge and information capability to help enhance teaching and learning for all students; and designs and maintains flexible and adaptable physical learning facilities that promote and support 21st century learning environments.

Capabilities as a basis for planning leadership formation programs

The type of leadership capabilities just discussed have also been approximated in other research. Flintham (2003, pp. 20–21), reporting on his research in England which partly focused on the development of head teachers' capacity to exercise spiritual and moral leadership, identified the following growth areas: growth in confidence; growth in self-awareness; growth in risk-taking capacity; and growth in 'being' rather than 'doing'. For me, these growth areas support the idea of a formation approach that includes many of the leadership capabilities just discussed. In the conclusions to his research, Flintham (2003, p. 22) recommended stages of head teacher development (based on the work of West-Burnham, 2002) which progress from '. . . external authenticity derived from the trappings and symbols of power to internal authenticity', which is, primarily, derived from reflection, ethical purpose, wisdom and transcendence, the latter leading to the discovery of the fully authentic self. The work of West-Burnham and Flintham would appear to support a major claim in this book: that educational leaders need, first and foremost, to become capable and authentic human beings.

It is not my intention to suggest here a specific blueprint and content for an educational leadership formation program based on the leadership capabilities just discussed. The challenge of developing such a blueprint constitutes a work in progress for this author. This challenge is also there for others who have responsibility for the development and delivery of educational leadership development programs.

I will, however, provide some general suggestions for a possible philosophy, formation process, and preferred modes of delivery for such a formation program.

There are a number of excellent books and numerous websites on various aspects of the development and delivery of effective professional development programs. The purpose here is to provide a particular perspective on forming educational leaders by recommending a focus on ethical decision-making and leadership capabilities in such programs.

Possible structures

Leaders' capabilities cannot be formed overnight. I do believe, however, that all leaders can 're-form' and this reforming must start with personal reflection and critique, complemented by opportunities to engage with colleagues and mentors in deliberately constructed and creative learning experiences. While I admit that some people in leadership positions may have fixed mindsets and paradigms and all will have their particular personality types, I passionately believe that all leaders can with time, effort and sincere commitment greatly improve themselves as human beings, educators and educational leaders.

Leadership formation programs should engage leaders in purposeful educative processes over substantial time periods. While the right time to start to form educational leaders is when teachers first enter the profession, I will focus mostly here on principals as leaders and on those aspiring to formal leadership positions in schools, for example, deputy/assistant principals, department heads and subject/curriculum coordinators.

Programs should be structured over a period of at least two years, with planned intermittent episodes of face-to-face engagement (2–3 days at a time), and action learning periods in the workplace based on experiential learning from problem-based project work (approximately 2 months each period). These could be supported by the use of customised interactive websites to generate a continuing dialogue on, and critique of, key issues and challenges; opportunities for participants to partner and network with colleagues both inside and outside of their systems; and one or more high profile summits or conferences at which participants can showcase their learning.

Within such a structure, a number of processes can be used, which are particularly well suited to a formation approach.

Possible processes

Several processes have been shown to be effective in recent attempts to form leaders, rather than train them. These are discussed below.

Learning projects

The 'Leaders transforming learners and learning' (LTLL) pilot project (2005–06), referred to earlier, engaged teams of educational leaders (4 per team) from nine schools in generating and implementing *learning projects* over an eighteen-month period. The main focus of this pilot project was on the formation of authentic leaders who can develop schools in which authentic learning takes place. The approach adopted by each team is a problem-based learning approach. In the eighteen-month period all nine teams meet as a group in face-to-face sessions on five occasions (to plan, critique, refine and evaluate their learning experiences). Between these meetings the teams are busy implementing their learning projects, and they meet frequently as individual school teams and also with other teams nearby. Participants have, to date, been introduced to cutting-edge literature on authentic leadership, authentic pedagogy, and authentic learning. In fact, Starratt's (2004a) *Ethical leadership* is recommended as essential reading. Discussions on ethics and ethical applications are frequent.

Throughout the eighteen months university project staff and selected personnel from the school systems help support and mentor those involved in the learning projects. A customised interactive website operates to provide a forum for continuing dialogue on and critique of the learning projects. Participants and mentors have judged this approach to be highly effective.

Face-to-face sessions

Dempster, Freakley and Parry (2001b) have proposed the concept of 'communities of ethical inquiry' as a framework for the professional development of educational leaders, especially principals, to better prepare them for making ethical decisions in unanticipated, novel or unfamiliar situations. Dempster (2001, p. 11), in *The ethical development of school principals*, found that the most strongly preferred modes of delivery for professional development related to ethical decision-making for school principals were 'those that involved interaction with others in face-to-face settings', closely followed by 'professional networking' and 'mentoring'. He recommended (p. 18) that principals should engage in face-to-face dialogue on complex ethical dualities that challenge their professional values and 'test their personal professional values against real-life scenarios'. A distinctive feature of such an approach to professional development 'is the use of vignettes of ethical issues . . . for the purposes of learning about the processes of applied ethical inquiry'.

It would appear, therefore, that apart from experiential learning on the job, leaders are best formed and nurtured in face-to-face situations. The content and processes used in these sessions can then be followed by further exploration and experiential learning in the workplace over time. Such a format strongly suggests that educational leaders should be brought together outside the workplace for face-to-face interactive sessions, to provide opportunities to reflect on, critique and analyse complex issues and tensions. Case studies, deliberately constructed from real-life critical incidents in schools, requiring real-life leadership attributes and capabilities for their critique, analysis and resolution, are recommended.

Development and analysis of complex cases

The consideration of cases that highlight value dualities and ethical tensions, similar to those described and discussed in earlier chapters, can be key learning tools for educational leaders. Wildy *et al.* (2001), drawing on the research of Dempster, Freakley and Parry (2001a), recommend that programs of study and discussions about contestable values dualities 'have the potential to contribute substantially to shaping and confirming the professional values faced by principals and teachers in their everyday work'. Wildy *et al.* (2001) have noted 'the power of the case that is grounded in everyday recognisable problems and dilemmas to stimulate reflection on practice'.

The Lutheran Leadership Development Project (LLDP, 2005) has shown that part of the process can be the construction of complex cases, drawn from real-life experiences. It is best to encourage small groups to pool their experiences and craft multidimensional and tension-filled cases, like the ones reported and discussed in chapter 3. The reflection, critique and analysis of issues and tensions required for the construction of complex cases is a productive learning experience in itself. The swapping of these cases across groups for analysis constitutes another important learning opportunity. Cases generated by the learning groups themselves will be more relevant and more meaningful to their work situations, as was the case in the LLDP.

Case studies encourage participants in formation programs to reflect on their theories and practice of leadership. Another useful tool, with similar outcomes, was used to great effect in the LLDP (2005). It was referred to as a 'leadership development portfolio'.

Leadership development portfolio

The focus of the LLDP was on profiling aspiring leaders to determine their leadership development needs. These aspiring leaders were challenged to construct a leadership development portfolio. This involved a two-month long opportunity to reflect on and critique their leadership strengths and areas needing improvement. Participants in the project were also required to formally analyse two complex case studies and send their analysis, together with the completed portfolio, to the project mentors.

The portfolio and the analysis of cases, overall, generated in-depth data, which provided useful indicators of their leadership development needs. A leadership development profile was developed for each aspiring leader and these profiles assisted in creating customised development pathways and programs for each participant.

The development portfolio – which actually turned out to be a deep learning experience for participants – was constructed around six key areas. These were:

1 **Personal reflection on leadership experience and achievements** – This included questions about why they chose education as a career; professional experiences and achievements that had given them most satisfaction; educators who had a significant impact on them and why; the special gifts they bring to their leadership; and their major contributions to leadership in their school communities.

2 **Personal reflection on the dimensions of leadership that were part of their system's leadership framework** – This included questions related to visionary leadership; authentic leadership; educative leadership; organisational leadership; and community leadership.

3 **Personal reflection on capabilities required for effective leadership in their school/system** – This included questions related to the capabilities discussed earlier in this chapter. Each of the individual capabilities listed under the four categories (personal, relational, professional and organisational) was plotted on a 5-point Likert scale and each participant was asked to evaluate whether it was a strength (5 on the scale) or an area needing development (1 on the scale).

4 **Reflection on personal experience of best practice** – This included requests for examples of best practice in leadership, i.e. when they felt they were at their best; and reflection on

this best practice to encourage learning about their capacity for leadership.

5 **Reflection on, and critique of, their priorities for personal and professional leadership development** – This included comments on the first four areas of reflection; it asked them to identify their leadership strengths and personal and professional development needs in terms of leadership attributes and capabilities – it constituted their development profile, including their strengths and needs.

6 **Comment and critique by the school principal on number 5, on strengths and needs** – The principal, in consultation with the aspiring leader, was asked to analyse the aspirant's profile and make recommendations for his/her future personal and professional development for leadership.

While participants' responses to the portfolio and case studies constitute examples only of simulated performance, they are proposed as a valid approach to evaluate an educational leader's '. . . capacity to practice and understand his or her craft as well as to communicate the reasons for professional decisions to others' (Clarke, Wildy & Louden, 2000, based on their use of in-basket and mini-cases). Those who analysed the cases and completed their portfolios were required to: analyse situations involving conflicting principles, values and ethics; exercise contextualised leadership judgement (in the context of their school); and 'create an action plan describing the actions needing to be implemented and justify the actions intended to be taken' (Clarke, Wildy & Louden, 2000, p. 6).

Wildy *et al.* (2001) claim that mini-cases and in-basket exercises constitute a valid approach to evaluating a principal's capacity to practise and understand his or her craft. The research team in the LLDP concluded that this approach, with some modifications (portfolio was substituted for in-basket activities), could generate accurate, relevant, meaningful and useful snapshots of where participants were in their leadership development.

Analysis of life stories

I have a very high regard for the lessons to be learned from studying the lives of people who have known what it means to struggle and succeed, often against the odds. In Australia, the ABC network produce a television program called 'Australian Story' (http://www.abc.net.au/austory/). This program features ordinary and extraordinary Australians and the human drama in the lives they have led. Usually it depicts 'normal' human beings as they experience the highs and lows, the agony and the ecstasy, the trials and tribulations, the successes and failures in their lives. Most whose lives are featured demonstrate great moral fibre, authenticity and resiliency. I have watched these programs with great interest, hoping that I can re-form and transform myself to be more like them.

A similar source of inspiration and moral witness is the video biography series 'Famous Lives' (1999, Design REEL Corporation). I take great hope from the biographies of Nelson Mandela and Lech Walesa in particular. Their stories provide me with benchmarks to which I can aspire. Mandela, especially, has taught me that it is important to be humble, tolerant, forgiving, optimistic and hopeful.

There are numerous other sources that can be used in formation programs. Great literary biographies are obvious sources. Readers of this book will, no doubt, have their own favourites. Another favourite of mine is *Lives of Moral Leadership* by Coles (2000). In his introduction (p. xi) he states that we need moral heroes who can inspire us to purposeful action and also to want to take on leadership ourselves, in order to inspire others. He concludes that while we need moral leaders and leadership, 'the need for moral inspiration is ever present'.

Bennett's (1993) *The book of virtues: A treasury of great moral stories* presents a large number of inspiring stories organised around the themes of self-discipline, compassion, responsibility, friendship, work, courage, perseverance, honesty, loyalty, and faith. While these stories are aimed primarily at children, they provide insights into moral living that can benefit us all. Klein's (2003) book *A year with C. S. Lewis: Daily readings from his classic works* is inspirational with numerous topics relevant to a formation program.

There are, no doubt, many other ways and means of engaging educational leaders in leadership formational processes and activities. I have tried in this chapter to provide a philosophy and framework, as well as some suggestions for structure, processes and content. I believe that the leadership capabilities constitute a useful starting point.

Bringing it all back home

There is a new energy abroad that is calling, perhaps crying out, for leaders of our systems and institutions to be more authentic and capable. I have tried in this book to make a case to answer the call. I also believe that we have a great window of opportunity in education to lead the way, in fact, to show it can be done. I have made a case in chapter 8 and in this chapter for the need to move beyond competency-based views of leaders and leadership and adopt a formational perspective based on leadership capabilities.

Before submitting this book for publication, I received a copy of *Sustainable leadership* by Hargreaves and Fink (2006). In it, they argued that we need authentically sustainable leadership and change processes in our schools because traditional mechanical and hierarchical approaches have been wasteful, ineffective, and unsustainable (pp. 265–266). We need solutions based on sustainable leadership with moral purpose and integrity. To date, there has been considerable waste of the time and efforts of our teachers, leaders and students because of top-down changes that lack authenticity in leadership. We can, they stated, especially, 'tolerate no more wasted lives among our children' (p. 273).

I invite you to join me in becoming part of the solution.

Key ideas for reflection

The starting point for the development of capable and authentic educational leaders is personal transformation. As Senge *et al.* (2004, p. 215) have suggested, there appears to be a growing gap in many organisations between our power and our wisdom, and we must find ways of reversing it by enhancing human development and wisdom.

I suggested earlier that formation programs for educational leaders will be judged to be successful if they assist educational systems and schools to develop the capabilities of their leaders, thereby helping them to make a difference in their sphere of influence in education and in life.

A number of leadership capabilities, grouped into four categories – personal, relational, professional and organisational – were proposed in this chapter to form a basis for leadership formation programs. Developing leadership formation programs built around these capabilities remains a challenge.

Questions for reflection

You may wish to revisit again the critical incident or case you developed at the end of chapter 3 and refined through reflections and actions suggested at the end of other chapters. Carefully analyse your case, from both a capabilities and a formation perspective, by critically responding to the following questions:

- What are the key leadership challenges in this case?
- What key leadership capabilities are required to help resolve these challenges?
- What elements or content would you include in a leadership formation program designed to meet your needs, especially considering the leadership capabilities you have just identified?
- What formation processes or methodology would you select to help 'form' these leadership capabilities?

References

Andrews, D., Crowther, F., Hann, L. & McMaster, J. (2002) 'Teachers as leaders: re-imaging the profession'. *The Practising Administrator* 1.

Bazeley, P. & Richards, L. (2000) *The NVivo qualitative project book.* London: Sage.

Beck, U. & Beck-Gernsheim, E. (2002) *Individualization*, London: Sage.

Beckner, W. (2004) *Ethics for educational leaders.* Boston: Allyn & Bacon.

Begley, P. & Johansson, O. (1998) 'The values of school administration: Preferences, ethics and conflicts'. *The Journal of School Leadership* 8, 4: 399–422.

Benjamin, M. (1990) *Splitting the difference: Compromise and integrity in ethics and politics.* Lawrence, KA: University Press of Kansas.

Bennett, W.J. (1993) *The book of virtues: A treasury of great moral stories.* Melbourne: Bookman Press.

Bhindi, N. & Duignan, P. (1997) 'Leadership for a new century: authenticity, intentionality, spirituality and sensibility'. *Educational Management and Administration* 25, 2: 117–132.

Birch, C. & Paul, D. (2003) *Life and work: Challenging economic man.* Sydney: UNSW Press.

Bogue, E.G. (1994) *Leadership by design: Strengthening integrity in higher education.* San Francisco: Jossey-Bass.

Breton, D. & Largent, C. (1996) *The paradigm conspiracy: Why our social systems violate human potential – and how we can change them.* Minnesota: Center City, Hazelden.

Bridges, W. (1995) *Managing transitions: Making the most of change.* London: Nicholas Brealey.

Buckley, M.J. (1997) 'The Catholic University and the promise inherent in its identity'. In J.M. O'Keefe (ed.), *Catholic higher education at the turn of the century.* Boston: Boston College & Garland Publishing.

Burns J.M. (1978) *Leadership.* New York: Harper & Row.

Cairns, L. (1998) 'The capable teacher: The challenge of the 21st century'. Paper presented at the 28th Annual Conference, Australian Teacher Education Association, Melbourne.

Chesterton, P. & Duignan, P. (2004) *Evaluation of the national trial of the IDEAS Project.* Report to DEST. Sydney: ACU National.

Clark, S.R.P., Wildy, H. & Louden, W. (2000) *Assessing principals' performance: A research agenda.* Edith Cowan University, Mount Lawlor Campus W.A. 6050.

Coles, R. (2000) *Lives of moral leadership.* New York: Random House.

Concise Oxford dictionary (1984) Oxford: Oxford University Press. 7th edn.

Conger, J.A. & Associates. (1994) *Spirit at work: Discovering the spirituality in leadership.* San Francisco: Jossey-Bass.

Covey, S. (1992) *Principle-centred leadership.* New York: Simon & Schuster.

Crowther, F., Hann, L. & Andrews, D. (2002a) 'Rethinking the role of the school principal: Successful school improvement in the postindustrial era'. *The Practising Administrator* 24, 2.

Crowther, F., Kaagan, S.S., Ferguson, M. & Hann, L. (2002b) *Developing teacher leaders: How teacher leadership enhances school success.* Thousand Oaks, CA: Sage Publications.

d'Arbon, T., Duignan, P. & Duncan, D. (2003) 'Planning for future leadership of schools: An Australian study', *Journal of Educational Administration* 40, 5: 468–485.

Darling-Hammond, L. (1999) 'Educating teachers: The Academy's greatest failure or its most important future?' *Academe* 85, 1.

Dempster, N. (2001) *The ethical development of school principals.* Brisbane: Griffith University Centre for leadership & management in education.

Dempster, N., Freakley, M. & Parry, L. (2001a) 'The ethical climate of public schooling under new public management'. *International Journal of Leadership in Education* 4, 1: 1–12.

Dempster, N., Freakley, M. & Parry, L. (2001b) 'Principals' professional development in ethical decision-making through case study'. Paper presented at the twenty-first annual conference of the International Society for Teacher Education, Kuwait.

Deveterre, R.I. (1995) *Practical decision making in health care ethics: Cases and concepts.* Washington, DC: Georgetown University Press.

Duignan, P. (2002a) 'Formation of authentic educational leaders for Catholic schools'. In D. Duncan & D. Riley (eds.), *Leadership in Catholic education.* Melbourne: Harper Collins, pp. 172–183.

Duignan, P. (2002b) 'The Catholic educational leader: Defining authentic leadership: veritas, caritas, gravitas'. Paper presented at the International Conference on Catholic Educational Leadership, ACU, Sydney.

Duignan, P. (2004a) 'Forming capable leaders: From competencies to capabilities'. *New Zealand Journal of Educational Leadership* 19, 2: 5–12.

Duignan, P. (2004b) *The insight and foresight of Bill Walker: Motorcycle maintenance 30 years on (1974–2004)*. Australian Council for Educational Leadership Monograph Series, No. 35, November.

Duignan, P. (2005) 'Formation of capable leaders to lead schools in challenging times'. Paper prepared for the Microsoft New Zealand Inaugural Distinguished Travelling Scholar. Sydney: ACU National.

Duignan, P. & Bezzina, M. (2004) 'Leadership and learning: Influencing what really matters'. Presentation at the Teacher Education Council Conference, ACU National, Strathfield,

Duignan, P. & Bhindi, N. (1997) 'Authenticity in leadership: An emerging perspective'. *Journal of Educational Administration*, 35, 3 & 4: 195–209.

Duignan, P. & Burford, C. (2002) 'Preparing educational leaders for the paradoxes and dilemmas of contemporary schooling'. Paper presented at the British Educational Research Association Annual Conference, UK: Exeter.

Duignan, P., Butcher, J., Spies-Butcher, B. & Collins, J.F. (2005) *Socially responsible indicators for policy, practice and benchmarking in service organisations*. Sydney: ACU National.

Duignan, P. & Collins, V. (2003) 'Leadership challenges and ethical dilemmas in front-line organisations'. In M. Bennett, C. Crawford & M. Cartwright (eds.), *Effective educational leadership*. London: Open University Press, pp. 281–294.

Duignan, P. & Macpherson, R.J.S. (1992) *Educative leadership: A practical theory for new administrators and managers*. London: Falmer Press.

Duignan, P. & Macpherson, R.J.S. (1993) 'Educative leadership: A practical theory'. *Educational Administrative Quarterly*, 29, 1: 8–33.

Duignan, P. & Marks, W. (2003) 'From competencies to capabilities: Developing shared leadership in schools'. Paper presented at the Australian Council for Educational Leadership Annual Conference, Sydney.

Duignan, P. *et al.* (2003) *SOLR project: Contemporary challenges and implications for leaders in frontline human service organisations*. Sydney: ACU National.

Elmore, R. (2000) *Building a new structure for school leadership.* Washington, DC: The Albert Shanker Institute.

English, A.W. (1995) 'The double-headed arrow: Australian managers in the context of Asia'. Unpublished doctoral thesis, University of New England.

Flintham, A. (2003) *Reservoirs of hope: Spiritual and moral leadership in head teachers.* National College for School Leadership (NCSL) Practitioner Enquiry Report, Nottingham: NCSL.

Fourre, C. (2003) *Journey to justice: Transforming hearts and schools with Catholic social teaching.* Washington, DC: National Catholic Educational Association.

Fullan, M. (1993) *Change forces: Probing the depths of educational reform.* London: Falmer Press.

Fullan, M. (2001) *Understanding change: Leading in a culture of change.* San Francisco: Jossey-Bass.

Fullan, M. (2003) *The moral imperative of school leadership.* Thousand Oaks, CA: Corwin Press.

Gatto, J.T. (1992) *Dumbing us down: The hidden curriculum of compulsory schooling.* Philadelphia: New Society Publishers.

Giddens, A. (1998) *The third way.* Cambridge, UK: Policy Press.

Gilligan, C. (1982) *In a different voice: Psychological theory and women's development.* Cambridge, MA: Harvard University Press.

Goleman, D., Boyatzis, R. & McKee, A. (2003) *The new leaders.* London: Time Warner Paperbacks.

Gronn, P.C. (2000) 'Distributed properties: A new architecture for leadership'. *Educational Management and Administration*, 28, 3: 317–338.

Groome, T. (1998) *Educating for life: A spiritual vision for every teacher and parent.* Allen, TX: Thomas More.

Gross, S.J. & Shapiro, J.P. (2005) *Our new era requires a new DEEL: Towards democratic ethical educational leadership.* Philadelphia: Temple University.

Halpern, B.L. & Lubar, K. (2003) *Leadership presence: Dramatic techniques to reach out, motivate, and inspire.* New York: Gotham Books.

Handy, C. (1994) *The empty raincoat: Making sense of the future.* London: Random House.

Handy, C. (1997) *The hungry spirit: Beyond capitalism.* London: Hutchinson.

Hargreaves, A. & Fink, D. (2006) *Sustainable leadership.* San Francisco: Jossey-Bass.

Hargreaves, A. & Fullan, M. (1998) *What's worth fighting for: Working together for your school.* Hawthorne: ACEA Paperbacks.

Harris, A. (2002) 'Distributed leadership in schools: Leading or misleading'. Keynote paper presented at the BELMAS annual conference, Birmingham, England.

Hede, A. & Wear, R. (1993) 'An empirical investigation of Australian political leadership'. Paper presented to the Australian Political Science Association Annual Conference, Monash University.

Heft, J.L. & Bennett, S.J. (2004) *The courage to lead: Catholic identity – diversity*. Washington, DC: National Catholic Educational Association.

Heifetz, R.A. (1994) *Leadership without easy answers*. Cambridge, MA: Harvard University Press.

Hesburgh, T.M. (1994) (ed.), *The challenge and promise of a Catholic university*. Notre Dame, IN: University of Notre Dame Press.

Hodgkinson, C. (1991) *Educational leadership: The moral art*. Albany, NY: University of New York Press.

Institute for Educational Leadership (2001) *Leadership for student learning: Redefining the teacher as leader*. School Leadership for the 21st Century Initiative: A Report of the Task Force on Teacher Leadership, Washington, DC, April.

Josephson, M. (2002) *Making ethical decisions*. Los Angeles: Josephson Institute of Ethics.

Kaplan, R. & Norton, D. (1996) *Balanced scorecard: Translating strategy into action*. Boston: Harvard Business School Press.

Keane, J. (2003) *Global civil society?* Cambridge, UK: Cambridge University Press.

Kelly, T. (2000) 'Researching Catholicity at Australian Catholic University', Draft paper, ACU Sub-Faculty of Theology.

Kidder, R.M. (1995) *How good people make tough choices: Resolving the dilemmas of ethical living*. New York: William Morrow.

Klein, P.S. (2003) *A year with C.S. Lewis*. London: HarperCollins.

Kohlberg, L. & Turiel, E. (1971) 'Moral development and moral education'. In G. Lesser (ed.), *Psychology and educational practice*. Glenview, IL: Scott Foresman.

Little, A.D. (1997) *Managing change – the Australian experience: Survey results*. Sydney: Arthur D. Little International.

LLDP (2005) *Lutheran leadership development project*, ACU National: Flagship for Creative & Authentic Leadership (www.acu.edu.au/research/flagshipcel).

LTLL Project (2005–06) *Leaders transforming learners and learning*, Sydney, ACU National.

MacIntyre, A. (1985) *After virtue*. London: Duckworth.

Marks, W. (2002–03) From competency training to leadership capabilities. NSWDET workshops with school principals.

Marks, W. (2003) 'Effective leadership preparation programs'. Frank Farrell Award Report, Sydney: DET.

NCSL (2006) *Five pillars of distributed leadership.* National College for School Leadership Monograph 3.1, Distributed leadership. Nottingham: NCSL. www.ncsl.org.uk/distributedleadership

Newman, F. & Wehlage, G. (1995) *Successful school restructuring.* Alexandria, VA: Association for Supervision and Curriculum Development.

Newman, J.H. (Cardinal) (1915) *On the scope and nature of university education.* London: J.M. Dent.

Nussbaum, M. (2000) 'Aristotle in the workplace'. In M. Tobias, J.P. Fitzgerald & D. Rothenberg (eds.), *A parliament of minds: Philosophy for a new millennium.* Albany, NY: State University of New York Press, pp. 30–45.

O'Donohue, J. (1997) *Anam cara.* London: Bantam Press.

Onsman, H. (2003) *The uncertain art of management.* AIM Management Series. Sydney: McGraw Hill.

Parry, K.W. (1998) 'Grounded theory and social process: A new direction for leadership research'. *Leadership Quarterly*, 9, 1: 885–905.

Pearce, C.L. & Sims, H.P. Jr. (2000) 'Shared leadership: Towards a multi-level theory of leadership'. *Advances in the Interdisciplinary Studies of Work Teams*, 7: 115–139.

Piaget, J. (1965) *The moral judgment of the child.* New York: The Free Press.

Pirsig, M. (1992) *Lila: An inquiry into morals.* London: Corgi Books.

Power, F.C., Higgins, A. & Kohlberg, L. (1989) *Lawrence Kohlberg's approach to moral education.* New York: Columbia University Press.

Rebore, R.W. (2001) *The ethics of educational leadership.* New Jersey: Prentice-Hall.

Santiago, P. (2001) *Education policy analysis.* Paris: OECD.

Schaef, A.W. (1987) *When society becomes an addict.* San Francisco: Harper.

Scott, G. (2003) *Learning principals: Leadership capabilities and learning research in the New South Wales Department of Education and Training.* Sydney: University of Technology, Sydney.

Seddon, T. (2002) 'Redesigning collective educational capacity: From integrated public systems to capacity building enterprises'. *Australian Education Researcher*, 29, 2.

Selznick, P. (1992) *The moral commonwealth: Social theory and the promise of community.* Los Angeles: University of California Press.

Senge, P., Scharmer, C.O., Jaworski, J. & Flowers, B.S. (2004) *Presence: Human purpose and the field of the future.* Cambridge, MA: the Society for Organisational Learning Inc.

Sergiovanni, T.J. (1992) *Moral leadership: Getting to the heart of school improvement.* New York: Jossey-Bass.

Sergiovanni, T.J. (1999) *Rethinking leadership: A collection of articles.* Arlington Heights, IL: Skylight Training & Publishing.

Sergiovanni, T.J. (2000) *The life world of leadership: Creating culture, community and personal meaning in our schools.* San Francisco: Jossey Bass Publishers.

Shapiro, J.P. & Stefkovich, J.A. (2005) *Ethical leadership and decision making in education: Applying theoretical perspectives to complex dilemmas,* 2nd edn. New York: Lawrence Erlbaum.

Silins, H. & Mulford, B. (2002) 'Leadership and school results'. In K. Leithwood & P. Hallinger (eds.), *International handbook of educational leadership and administration.* Norwell, MA: Kluwer, pp. 561–612.

Singer, P. (1979) *Practical ethics.* Cambridge: Cambridge University Press.

Solomon, R.C. (1993) *Ethics and excellence: Cooperation and integrity in business.* Oxford: Oxford University Press.

Sommerville, M. (2000) *The ethical canary: Science, society and the human spirit.* Ringwood, Victoria: Penguin.

Spillane, J.P., Halverson, R. & Diamond, J.B. (2001) 'Investigating school leadership practice: A distributed perspective'. *Educational Researcher,* April, pp. 23–28.

Spry, G. (2004) *A framework for leadership in Queensland Catholic schools.* QCEC/ACU Research Project. Email: g.spry@mcauley.acu. edu.au

Spry, G. & Duignan, P. (2003) 'Framing leadership in Queensland Catholic schools'. Paper presented at the NZARE AARE Conference, Auckland, NZ.

Starratt, R.J. (1994) *Building an ethical school: A practical response to the moral crisis in schools.* London: The Falmer Press.

Starratt, R.J. (2003) *Centering educational administration.* Mahwah, NJ: Lawrence Erlbaum.

Starratt, R.J. (2004a) *Ethical leadership.* San Francisco: Jossey Bass.

Starratt, R.J. (2004b) PowerPoint presentation for Parramatta Principals Seminar. Parramatta, NSW: Catholic Education Office.

Stephenson, J. (1992) 'Capability and quality in higher education'. In J. Stephenson & S. Weil (eds.), *Quality in learning: A capability approach in higher education.* London: Kogan Page, pp. 1–7.

Stephenson, J. (1994) 'Capability and competence: Are they the same and does it matter?' *Capability*, 1, 1: 3–4.

Stephenson, J. (2000) *Corporate capability: Implications for the style and direction of work-based learning.* Working Paper 99–14. University Technology Sydney, Research Centre for Vocational Education and Training, pp. 1–16.

Surowiecki, J. (2005) *The wisdom of crowds.* New York: Anchor Books.

Taylor, C. (1989) *Sources of the self: The making of the modern identity.* Cambridge, MA: Harvard Universal Press.

Taylor, C. (1991) *The ethics of authenticity.* Cambridge, MA: Harvard University Press.

Terry, R.W. (1993) *Authentic leadership: Courage in action.* San Francisco: Jossey Bass.

Townsend, T. (1998) 'The primary school in the future: Third world or third millennium?' In T. Townsend (ed.), *The primary school in changing times: The Australian experience.* London: Routledge.

Townsend, T. (1999) 'Leading in times of rapid change'. Keynote address at the Annual Conference of the Australian Secondary Principals Association, Canberra.

Turiel, E. (1983) *The development of social knowledge: Morality & convention.* New York: Cambridge University Press.

Vroom, V.H. & Yetton, P.W. (1973) *Leadership and decision making.* Pittsburgh, PA: Pittsburgh Press.

West-Burnham, J. (2002) 'Leadership and spirituality'. National College of School Leadership (NCSL) Leading Edge Seminar Thinkpiece. Nottingham: NCSL, July.

Wildy, H., Louden, W., Dempster, N. & Freakley, M. (2001) 'The moral dimensions of school principals' work: Standards, cases and social capital'. *Unicorn, Australian College of Educators*, 11: 1–15.

Williams, T. (Cardinal) (2000) 'The role of the principal in Catholic schools'. Presentation to the Association of Catholic Principals of NSW Annual Conference, Tamworth.

Index